BIDI-ROLLING IN RURAL DEVELOPMENT

BIDI-ROLLING
IN RURAL DEVELOPMENT

S. GIRIAPPA

2022
Daya Publishing House®
A Division of
Astral International Pvt. Ltd.
New Delhi – 110 002

First Published, 1987

Reprinted, 2022

ISBN: 9788170352068 (H.B.)

Published by : **Daya Publishing House®**
A Division of
Astral International Pvt. Ltd.
– ISO 9001:2015 Certified Company –
4736/23, Ansari Road, Darya Ganj
New Delhi-110 002
Ph. 011-43549197, 23278134
E-mail: info@astralint.com
Website: www.astralint.com

PREFACE

Rural development has assumed the role of the 'leading sector' in economic development in recent times. This is due to the fact that other sectors have not been able to support it integratively. The task of rural development process is manifold. It has to pull a sizeable proportion of population above the minimum poverty level. It has to emphasize on the under-developed sub-sectors in the rural system. Above all, it has to bring in an awareness amcng policy-makers, institutional agencies and the people at large as to the immediacy of abating the ills of poverty, inequality and inefficiency.

This study purports to highlight the role played by a specific rural sector like bidi-rolling with reference to its contribution to rural diversification, prosperity, employment and to the growth potential of the particular economic system. Also, the conditions of bidi labour, problems in bidi-rolling, etc. are considered in their due perspective. Developing a sector which has growth potential would quicken the process of rural development. Of course, the latter it possible only with basic structural changes and the present programmes may smoothen the process toward such a stage set-up. The success of rural development policy will largely depend on the creation and development of long-term growth potentialities.

This study was undertaken as a part of the SBI Chair programme. In the conduct of the study, the assistance rendered by M/s Sripathi K.P., Seetharam M., Sandhya V., Muktha Shet, the Mangalore University, various bidi manufacturers and bidi-rollers and others is amply acknowledged with thanks.

It is understood that the study may highlight the problems of bidi-rollers (say, that of women and child labour) in its proper perspective so that the policy-makers may draw useful guidelines for the development of that particular sector and complete institutionalisation of the rural system.

S. GIRIAPPA

LIST OF TABLES

Pages

CONTENTS

Balanced Smoke

Balanced smoke, unweary of health
Drives not the rollers onto stealth
Evil or bondage, little be the result
Of carping, branding and all iusult.
Long as smokers there, growers also be
Ergo, balance knot with naught.

S. GIRIAPPA

1

RURAL DEVELOPMENT

There exists a limit to which resources can be put into effective use to solve the basic need problem which is most crucial especially in the rural sector. From grow more food to the recent grow more wood campaign, all the programmes have aimed at providing more food, fuel and better lifestyle to the people. However, increasing population growth seems to be a liability also, besides being an asset. In rural area, labour intensive activities like domestic work, tending of livestock, collection of fuel, water and fodder, farm work and transport demand a large family norm. The man-land ratio is declining rapidly. More than half of the landholdings have become uneconomical. The intensity of mechanisation and fertiliser application would not be significant even by the turn of century. Added to this, realisation of improved irrigation resources is also limited. Hence, owing to resource and energy constraints, a priority treatment is required wherein low cost, high efficient appropriate technology has to be evolved and escalated throughout the rural areas so that they become sufficiently viable to develop.

When the theory of world economic growth which specified that there is only one model of development common to both developed and developing countries failed to deliver the deserved impact, alternative growth models were evolved to give importance to micro specificities. Plural development, endogenity, eco-development, etc. have been propagated in the case of developing economies and sectors that have been unable to be influenced by modern technology. The existence of technology versus non-technology sectors compels a stage of development which should initiate a negentorpic process wherein the non-technologised sectors also would develop along with technologised sectors. The belief that development of the latter at the cost of the former due to resource and infrastructure constraints would spill over the benefits has been nullified.

The initiation of community and rural development programmes in India has been directed toward improving the living conditions of the rural poor. This implies improvement in the local technology and selective application of exotic technology. Hence, rural development is an exercise in appropriate technology and micro-development process. The national programme of waste land development, realisation of better irrigation potential, development forestry, encouragement of bio-energies and renewable sources of energy, dry land farming and improved cultivation practices, etc. are some of the recent growth strategies adopted in this regard. It could be said that the advent of recent rural technology has been responsible for increasing growth rates found in many rural sectors.

However, the concept of rural development has been used in the context of removal of poverty in a short term notion to a large extent and when the long term perspective is missing, the concept can lead to dualistic growth structure. So, when the purpose for which the concept is to be used, i,e negation of dualistic growth is impaired, this will lead to pluralistic development patterns within the given sectors.

Integrated Rural Development Programme

The Integrated Rural Development Programme (IRDP) which has been in vogue in one form or the other since Independence, has underwent some structural changes from a notion of community participation mainly through village institutions to the later stage of area development and to the present-day micro-approach (specific target, micro-regional and sectoral development). The necessity to provide basic infrastructure, extension, training and asset-push programmes, etc. caused this change in fundamental policy perspective.

The importance of several rural programmes for developmental activities have been established since long. The creation of rural development society to coordinate work of different government departments and the involvement of various institutions (social, educational and voluntary) have had certain advantages and drawbacks as well. Different approaches—community, target group, village clusters, area, employment and social welfare in addition to the role of political economy—have common objectives of bringing the rural poor above the so-called illusory poverty line. As a matter of relative parlance, over 75 per cent of rural and 50 per cent of urban population could be treated as poor and non-viable. When the level of energy uptake either in thermal or alimentary sense is lower so as to accommodate a declining proportion of development population, it cannot be said that the particular break-away point is suggestive of any betterment in lifestyles. It is a question of inequalities which have arisen due to differences in endowment potentialities, and lack of infusion of modernisation elements to those who need the most. Both distributing justice and improving the living conditions of the poorest have in them the salient features of micro-development through decentralised local participation, where local participation would denote optimum utilisation of local resources—human, physical and environmental.

Evaluation as to the contribution of rural development strategies to the achievement of building a technologically progressive economy and to the realisation of a social order based on justice and equal opportunities for all have had mixed effects and implications. The role of Parkinson's Law in increasing government bureaucratic role and expenditure, institutional weakness, absence of multi-sectoral integrated thrust and the very nature of the programmes are some of the factors in poor absorption of the desired change. The problems faced in the identification of proper objectives, priorities, areas of operation, institutional coordination and coverage of specific types of beneficiaries have resulted in dilution of the programmes such that their real intensity has been eroded through the short-term objectives.

Target Group Approach

The rural poor constitute a 'target group' for whose benefit special programmes have been designed. The first major programme addressed to a target group of the rural poor was the small farmers and marginal farmers under the development programme initiated in the Fourth Plan. The IRDP is a more ambitious strategy for reducing poverty in our rural areas through the methodology tested under the SFDA programme. The target group of the IRDP consists of all rural families below the poverty line, viz. small farmers, marginal farmers, agricultural labourers, rural artisans, craftsmen, etc. Since the target group encompasses virtually half of all rural households, it is necessary to introduce a principle of selection within the target group itself. Under the IRDP, this is sought to be achieved by selecting the poorest among the poor first for providing assistance. A family with an annual income of Rs 3,500.00 or below is reckoned to be living below the poverty line. It is assumed that an average family consists of 5 members. Now though all poor rural families with an annual income of Rs 3,500.00 or less are eligible for assistance under the IRDP, families with the lowest income are to be provided assistance in the first instance.

The objective of the IRDP is to raise families of the rural poor above the poverty line through provision of assistance mainly in the form of productive assets. It is intended that the assistance should generate such substantial incremental income as to provide the beneficiary a standard of living which is well above the poverty line. The assistance is to be financed through subsidies provided by the government and loans advanced by the banking institutions. It is to be ensured that the families who have been assisted under this programme are provided adequate training and marketing and other support for making the investment truly effective and for preventing the families from slipping back into poverty.

The objective is to assist, on an average, 600 poor families per block per year and 3000 families per block during the Sixth Plan period. In this manner, 3 million families were assisted in a year and 15 million families in the course of the Sixth Plan in the country as a whole. The outlay on subsidy, etc. is Rs 35 lakhs per block during the Sixth Plan period. In 1981-82, the IRDP outlay per block was Rs 6 lakhs. This is being stepped up to Rs 8 lakhs from 1982-83. The outlay on IRDP in the Plan was Rs 1500 crores. This is shared on a 50:50 basis by the states and the Central Ministry. The credit requirement for IRDP was established to be Rs 3,000 crores during the Sixth Plan period. Thus, the IRDP envisaged an investment of about Rs 4,500 crores in the rural sector during the Sixth Plan. It is one of the largest single programmes in the entire plan and now it is included in the revised 20-point programme announced by the Prime Minister.

In the IRDP target group, the Scheduled Castes and Scheduled Tribes represent a very large proportion. It has, therefore, been laid down that priority should be accorded to the families of Scheduled Castes and Scheduled Tribes in providing assistance under this programme. The current target is to provide assistance in such a way that at least 30 per cent of all the families assisted are drawn from Scheduled Castes and Scheduled Tribes categories. Further, it is expected that at least 30 per cent of the investment made under this programme through subsidies and loans should also go to Scheduled Castes and Scheduled Tribes families. Since the Scheduled Caste and Schedule tribe population is not evenly distributed, the implementing agencies have been directed to attempt higher targets wherever it is practicable. These agencies have been advised to identify the concentration of Scheduled Caste and Scheduled Tribe families in their respective blocks and to attempt higher targets for the concerned blocks and districts.

While the SFDA programme was confined to agriculture, minor irrigation and animal husbandry programmes, the IRDP has a much broader coverage in terms of activities. Virtually any viable economic activity could be taken up under this programme. The selected activity should have the potential for generating substantial incremental income and the beneficiary should have the required interest in an aptitude for the activity. Potential beneficiaries are being provided training in the activities for which assistance is provided. On an average, four hundred families are to be provided assistance in agriculture and allied activities per block per year. Two hundred families per block per year are to be given assistance for non-agricultural occupations. In this manner, assistance for agriculturists, artisans, craftsmen and others is to be extended in a balanced manner to suit the needs of various categories of rural poor within the target group.

The IRDP is to be implemented through systematic block

level planning for resources development and employment generation for the benefit of the rural poor. Training is continuously being imparted to all categories of personnel involved in the Programme. The methodology implies preparation of a resource inventory, conduct of household surveys for identifying beneficiaries on the basis of their income, formulation of individual beneficiary-oriented schemes, provision of infrastructure support, establishment of linkages with other programmes, etc. This methodology is now being adopted by all the states. Annual Action Plans are to be drawn for each block. Similarly, a Five Year Perspective Plan is also to be drawn up for each block and each district. Almost all states have formulated an IRDP Annual Action Plan for the blocks. From 1982-83, the block plan under IRDP is insisted upon for every block in the country and Central assistance is being provided only to those agencies which have furnished their action plans to the State Governments and Central Ministry within a stipulated time.

It is assumed that infrastructure support for implementing the IRDP would be provided by the agencies already operating in the field. In the formulation of the State Plans, it is expected that the requirements of the IRDP would be given due consideration and the infrastructure would be adequately expanded and strengthened to meet the needs of the IRDP. However, a part of the IRDP outlay, limited to 10 per cent. is also allowed to be utilised for providing infrastructure support for the individual beneficiary-oriented programmes.

The IRDP is to be implemented in a coordinated manner whereby linkages are established with other ongoing programmes. The implementing agencies are expected to establish linkages for provision of raw material, marketing outlets, training, etc. There are a number of other programmes for the weaker sections currently under implementation. Such programmes are also aimed at the rural poor. The Special Component Plan for Scheduled Caste and Scheduled Tribal Sub-Plan, Minimum Needs Programme, etc. are to be linked effectively with the IRDP. Such an integrated approach will be necessary to ensure that the rural poor receive lasting benefits through this programme.

Subsidies are limited to 25 per cent of the capital cost for small farmers and 33.3 per cent of the capital cost for all other categories of beneficiaries. Tribal beneficiaries are provided subsidies to the extent of 50 per cent of the capital cost. This means that for every rupee provided by way of subsidy, loans to the extent of Rs 2 or Rs 3 would be required. Thus, the success of the IRDP will depend largely on the flow of credit. The credit requirements of the IRDP have been projected to the public sector lending institutions and Reserve Bank of India (RBI) and nationalised banks have already committed themselves to supporting this programme fully. In December 1981, the RBI issued further instructions to Scheduled banks on the steps to be taken in providing credit support for the IRDP. From a review of performance in various states, some specific operational problems have come to light. These are :

(a) *Security Cover* : It has been made clear beyond all doubt that, for loans up to Rs 5,000.00 no security cover shall be insisted upon. Since the beneficiary under the IRDP is, by definition, assetless, it would be more appropriate to look at the productivity of the proposed investment rather than the creditworthiness of the beneficiary. Bank officials at the lower levels are to be oriented towards this approach.

(b) *Size of Loans* : A few evaluation studies on IRDP have been completed and almost invariably it has been noticed that the size of the loans advanced to the average IRDP beneficiary is well below the optimum level. Small loans will not enhance the income of the beneficiary to the desired level. It is, therefore, necessary that substantial loans are provided.

(c) *Composite Family Plans* : Under the IRDP, often composite family plan with several components would be required to raise the family above the poverty line. It is noticed that banking institutions tend to accept financing of certain components to the exclusion of others. This will be counter-productive. All components are to be financed within a definite time frame so that the beneficiary receives adequate incremental incomes from all these components.

(d) *Loans to More than One Member of the Identified Family*: Sometimes in the composite family plan for an IRDP beneficiary, loans may be required for the head of the family and also for the dependants. Whether a loan is provided in the name of the head of the family or in the name of the dependants, it is to be understood that there is no ban on providing loans to more than one member of an identified family. Efforts are to be made to provide loans to the identified family in such a way that the combined income of all members of the family is large enough to raise the whole family above the poverty line.

(e) *Loans for SC & ST*: It is the uniform experience of implementing agencies that Scheduled Caste beneficiaries find it difficult to obtain loans from banks. Since they do not have landed property or other assets, Scheduled Caste beneficiaries tend to beat a disadvantage in obtaining loans. Further, they receive token loans of small amounts. A conscious effort to step up the provision of credit to the Scheduled Caste and Scheduled Tribe categories is required.

Evaluation of the Programmes

It has been estimated that about 16 million beneficiaries have received IRDP assistance at the close of Sixth Plan period. However, the evaluation studies conducted on the implementation of IRDP have revealed a number of deficiencies in the actual execution of the programme. Some of the findings are as follows:

(i) Identification of beneficiaries in most cases was not based on any surveys of regional plans.

(ii) Ineligible persons having annual family income of over Rs 3500.00 were selected.

(iii) Persons with inadequate knowledge about the activity to be undertaken without proper initiative were identified.

(iv) Activities financed were not supported by adequate infrastructural facilities and marketing support.

(v) A number of beneficiaries were provided assistance for activities like animal husbandry and dairy development without ensuring availability of supporting facilities, and

(vi) Norms prescribed by NABARD and the Reserve Bank regarding gestation period, total period of loan, provision of working capital and minimum size of unit were not followed.

Consequently, a large proportion of beneficiaries have not yet been able to cross the poverty line. As per a study conducted based on a sample survey of 8000 beneficiaries only Rs 500 crores out of the total Rs 4762 crores spent during the Sixth Plan period was properly used. The same study revealed that only 11 per cent of the beneficiaries could cross the revised poverty line.

The Programme Evaluation Organisation (PEO) of the Planning Commission conducted detailed study on IRDP covering a sample of 1,170 households in 33 districts of 16 states. The study has revealed some serious drawbacks in the administrative and organisational structure, planning and implementation of the IRDP. Adequate provision of necessary infrastructural or institutional and supporting facilities as well as more careful tailoring of the schemes to suit the differing conditions of various areas could greatly enhance the effectiveness and impact of the programme. The provision of the required infrastructural facilities to the beneficiary households in terms of adequate credit, supply of raw materials and other requirements, development of suitable linkages, training and upgradation of skills has a vital bearing on the successful operation of the programme. Together with a streamlined planning process, the more scientific preparation of perspective and annual action plans as well as devising of more appropriate schemes would have to receive due attention in future. The state level organisation lacked the required degree of support of the sectoral and subject matter specialists in the formulation of projects and schemes and in providing adequate technical guidance to the field staff. The block level machinery has been quite weak for providing appropriate and integrated delivery system. This was probably due to a dual control and multiplicity of other sectoral programmes being administered by the 'line departments' of the respective state-level organisations. The funds allotted for the creation of the infrastructural facilities to the extent of 10 per cent of the total allocation were not adequate.

Besides, different departments dealing with the various sectoral schemes lacked integrated and coordinated efforts in this direction. As regards preparation of the five year perspective plans, more than half of the states had, despite the emphasis in guidelines, not attempted such an exercise for the respective districts. Even in states where this exercise had been attempted, all the districts were not covered. There was no uniformity in the selection of families to be benefited under IRDP. The guidelines provided that the final selection of families should be based on a comprehensive household survey to ascertain their income, economic conditions and their preference for the benefit schemes or occupation. It was observed that such a survey was only conducted in four states and that too in some selected clusters of each block.

The National Bank for Agriculture and Rural Development (NABARD) study, in order to remove the drawbacks and to make the programme more effective, suggests the following measures :

(i) The role of the banks in the implementation of the programme needs to be improved.

(ii) There is an urgent need to augment the field staff in the rural branches of the banks engaged in the implementation of the programme so as to ensure proper planning and supervision over the end-use of credit and greater involvement in the identification of beneficiaries.

(iii) Bank should strictly follow the norms laid down by NABARD in respect of activities refinanced by it. The dilution of norms such as the prescription of shorter repayment periods, besides causing hardships to beneficiaries could also result in avoidable overdues.

(iv) The emphasis on achieving the target of assisting 600 families annually in each block has resulted in spreading the benefits of the programme too thin. Instead, it would be desirable to specify a target in terms of number of activities which could be assisted so that, depending on the requirements of each family, a package of activities could be provided.

(v) The identification of beneficiaries should preferably be done by a team comprising block and village functionaries and the bank staff. This would not only improve the quality of identification but also contribute to reducing the rate of rejection of applications by the banks. The incidence of coverage of ineligible families could also be minimised, if not eliminated totally.

(vi) In the selection of investment activity in individual cases, due consideration should be given to the skills and capabilities of the beneficiary and his preference.

(vii) It is necessary to ensure that no compromise is made in regard to the quality of assets as sub-standard assets financed under the programme have failed to confer any significant benefit to the poor.

(viii) The project approach to lending had not been adopted effectively while drawing up the annual block plans. It is necessary for the banks and the district administration to interact mutually in greater detail, in fixing the physical number of units in each activity for each block in the district, taking full note of the constraints arising from lack of potential, absence of infrastructural facilities and other factors so that the investments identified and assisted prove viable.

(ix) The amount of credit assistance and subsidy provided per beneficiary has not been adequate to acquire the right type, size and quality of assets required for generating the desired level of incremental income. Since the beneficiaries under the programme are the poorest of the poor, every effort has to be made to adhere to NABARD cost norms and avoid underfinancing.

(x) The banks and other concerned officials should impress upon the beneficiaries the need for adhering to the stipulated technical specifications of the investments, so that the risk of overcapitalisation or lower yield is avoided. Wherever necessary, even a second loan should be sanctioned to ensure sustained income accrual to the beneficiaries.

IRDP During the Seventh Plan

The new features of the programme aimed at improving implementation at the grassroot level, include the principle of selectivity in assisting the poorest of the poor, allocating funds on the basis of poverty incidence, increasing the number of women beneficiaries, setting up of District Supply and Marketing Societies (DSMS) and launching a new composite training scheme.

The government, it is understood, has decided to assist only one million beneficiaries every year, instead of three millions as in the Sixth Plan. These beneficiaries will be given a one-shot investment of Rs. 6000.00 per family. Besides, the previous three million beneficiaries would be given a supplementary dose of investment to bring them above poverty line.

Instead of uniform allocation of funds on a block-wise basis, it is now decided to provide funds to states based on the incidence of poverty. Since district-wise or block-wise data on poverty are not available the funds will be given on the basis of state-level statistics. This is expected to remove the anomaly by which some states do not get enough funds while other affluent states do not utilise even existing allocations. The need to improve infrastructural linkages for supply of raw materials and marketing of finished products in rural areas has been highlighted in the new plan. State governments will have to identify nodal organisation for supply and marketing purposes. In the absence of such organisation, they will have to establish District Supply and Marketing Societies for this purpose.

The level of women beneficiaries is also proposed to be increased. At the end of the Sixth Plan, only 8 per cent of the total beneficiaries were women. The target of coverage has now been raised to 30 per cent of total beneficiaries. A new scheme for training of beneficiaries will also be initiated which will include launching of new composite rural training at technical centres. Identification of beneficiaries which was found to be defective, is now proposed to be carried out with the assistance of peoples' representatives. Efforts will be made to create an awareness of benefits and right of beneficiaries of IRDP. Involvement of voluntary agencies will now be enhanced. This will enable taking up of family-oriented projects under the programme. Concurrent evaluation will now be carried out at the district level and monthly reports would have to be provided.

It is against this background that, when IRDP is being recast in the Seventh Plan and serious lacunae or deficiencies have been brought out by the studies of PEO and the NABARD, effective monitoring-cum-concurrent evaluation exercise becomes *sine qua non* during the implementation process. These aspects are briefly discussed hereunder and some relevant issues raised to draw the attention of the financiers, planners and administrators to set the system in order.

Implementation Process

The emphasis under IRDP is not on providing just some kind of assistance and achieving the target of an impressive number of beneficiaries but on providing substantial assistance to the identified participants which should increase their income to a significant extent so that they cross once and for all the poverty line. Thus, planning exercise has recognised the effective role the officials have to play in ensuring that the beneficiaries belonging to these target groups which have no access to the sources such as technical guidance, raw material, equipment, training, marketing, pricing of the products, credit, etc. get these facilities either under one umbrella (say, DIC, FSS, RMSC, etc.) or through a tie-up arrangement. In fact, experience reveals that these beneficiaries are given subsidy and credit for securing productive assets and then left to themselves for other needs. It is in this area that exploitative forces thrive.

Under IRDP, the Antyodaya approach has been recommended for selection of the beneficiaries under which the poorest of the poor are to be first selected. While small and marginal farmers have at least some land from which they can make out subsistence living, it is the landless labourer, released bonded labourer, tenant farmer, share-cropper and the like who are non-land based and have no regular source of income. They need to be identified and assisted under this programme through provision of package of schemes and services. Only then the subsidy, credit and other concessions would not be cornered by the relatively much better off families. In this case also, flaws in the identification process have enabled well-to-do families to take advantages in preference to the weakest of the weak.

The IRDP envisages monitoring of additional income generated in the case of each participant. In fact, this is the very basis of ensuring that the participant family derives regular income and crosses the poverty line once and for all. For this purpose more detailed monitoring at the block level is called for. It should be done in respect of each selected beneficiary. For this purpose, an identity-cum-monitoring card (IMC) has been devised. The information should be collected for each selected beneficiary. One copy should be with the beneficiary. Details of assistance provided should be entered in this book from time to time. All concerned agencies should be given this book so as to watch the progress of the beneficiary at every stage. Such a watch is kept till the beneficiary takes up his scheme and makes a success of it. Follow-up should normally be done for a period of two years after the beneficiary takes up his activity scheme by which time the beneficiary household would normally be able to cross the poverty line. However, this IMC has so far not been given to all the beneficiaries in every block and wherever it is given, no entries of additional production, income, employment, problems of developments, factors impeding the smooth implementation of the scheme, training needs, etc. have been made. In fact, benchmark survey of each and every family under this programme is a must. However, hardly any effort is made by the officials to monitor the progress of the scheme or activity pursued by the beneficiaries.

The lack of monitoring effort has, in a few cases, encouraged the beneficiaries to sell their assets in order to encash subsidy and credit and this has resulted in lower production of milk, eggs, etc. To enable the rural population to get the maximum benefit out of the various schemes being implemented under the IRDP, it would be necessary to acquaint the beneficiaries with the latest technology in the relevant fields by evolving suitable training programmes. Keeping this objective in view, training of beneficiaries who are introduced to new schemes, new occupations or modern technology is an important component of the IRDP. The full cost of training of beneficiaries may be provided out of this programme. Training is envisaged both in the agriculture and allied activities as well as in industrial activities. Training in agriculture and allied activities should be conducted in Gram Sevak Training Centres, Farmers' Training Centres, Krishi Vigyan Kendras and Agricultural Universities. Though such a provision as an integral part of the programme hardly any effort is made to train the beneficiaries, improve their skill and enhance productivity of resources and income.

While a comprehensive block plan will have to be prepared taking into account the objectives of a model block plan, the plan should be formulated taking into account the schemes that are eligible for assistance under this programme. The first step in the preparation of block level plans is the formulation of a resource inventory in respect of the selected block. The resource inventory should lead to certain specific action programmes which can be built into block level plan rather than merely stating possibilities, which may or may not be germane to the block level planning at all. To be specific the resource inventory should really concentrate on identifying potentialities which can be best exploited at the block level. Though this has been the basis and starting point for planning and implementation of programme, nowhere such a comprehensive plan has been prepared. What is being observed is that a list of beneficiaries identified under the programme is prepared and then application is filled up in respect of each beneficiary for a purpose or activity and this application is sent to the bank branch. Then the process of following up the applications starts. The earlier we formulate the comprehensive block plan, the better would be the end result.

The above discussion bring to a sharp focus the fact that there has been a wide gap between what was expected in the planning of IRDP and what has been attempted during the implementation process. This calls for urgent need for evolving an appropriate monitoring mechanism at the district level in order to continuously ascertain and verify whether the necessary functions or roles are played by the concerned agencies during implementation of the IRDP.

Institutional Agencies

Rural development is a long-term process, dynamic, diverse and demanding an integrative decentralised approach. The concept has undergone several changes according to given environment, policy priorities and institutional treatment. Several government and non-government evaluative studies as mentioned earlier have highlighted solution to the long-term perspective. Apathy of the implementing agencies and the sheer gigantic nature of the problem—all have contributed to the low performance of the programmes, especially in qualitative terms.

It has been long felt that an institutional approach to solve the problems of the rural sector in its entirety would be a right policy priority. The involvement of cooperatives, commercial banks, local organisations, educational and social institutions, besides various government departments, has been encouraged. An integration of the programmes with coordination by a single agency also has ushered in. It would seem that with all these, the concerned institutions have had mixed impacts on the different sectors of the rural economy and an effective role by them not only in plan formulation and execution, but also in monitoring, follow up and delivery of the relevant benefits is yet to be achieved satisfactorily. This calls for an efficient institutional development and positive commitment into the local specifics.

Evaluation of performance of the institutional agencies working in the field of rural development can be attempted in two ways. One is to evaluate the programme itself—how far it is amenable for involvement of the agencies in an amiable environment (meaning without clash of objectives and priorities). The other way would be to evaluate the working of the agencies in ushering in a workable local environment. One would feel that a via media would be just solution. With this, it should be possible to establish a nexus between the local environment and the change agents working to transform it.

Currently, the various rural programmes are coordinated by the Rural Development Society at the district level and eleven other institutions (government and non-government) have links with it in the execution of the programmes. In this, there is bound to be certain misunderstanding or clashes between the different agencies and it is paramount that specialised distribution of work to the agencies, depending on their resource allocations may be a workable policy perspective. Also, owing to inter-play of different technology levels, different sectors get varied sorts of treatment. The gap in technology escalation has to be reduced by the specialised working nature of the agencies. The question of technology transfer calls for a corresponding development of infrastructures without which neither the quality of the technology nor of the rural people can be improved. In properly identifying the objectives, priorities. beneficiaries and the areas to be developed, the agencies should develop an integrated way of working to justify their existence. Perhaps, encouragement by government and local environment becomes an essential element for a smooth functioning toward this. Such working is not an end itself, only a means toward further achievement. Here, we may allude to the perception of the government as to the essentiality of the non-government institutions owing to their better rapport with the local situation. Of course, science and technology have been much politicized in recent times and a better assessment of the same could be through an effective public participation. Herein lies the approach of the agencies—they should gear up the local environment toward awareness of the problem and the necessity to ameliorate it largely by themselves at least in the later stages of development.

We may cite the case of subsidies in initiating a process of development. No doubt, subsidies have played their role (not only in developing but also in developed systems) in mitigating the problems, especially of the poor. But subsidies happen to be a short-run solution and sooner or later, they have to be transformed into a growth-oriented incentive system which could try to strike a balance between the working of government, the different agencies and the local specifics themselves. Development cannot subsist only on reliefs (one is reminded of the oft-quoted jargon; slogans cannot be substitutes for solutions) and a long-term building up of infrastructure and incentives would be an answer. The agencies, in their part, can work toward that direction so that the government mechanism becomes receptive to such a process. A synthesis between different disciplines, qualitative training, understanding of the local environment—all would work toward achieving the required level of growth of the different sectors and transforming the poor.

Since the nature of the rural problem is so complex that the solution would be long-ranging, time-consuming and all-round. A better policy would be to assign the agencies their due role in the areas best fitted for them under a balanced control system so that such a decentralised way would develop the institutions (institutions building upon institutions) in a way best suited to the local environment. There may be lapses on the part of the agencies by striding out of the objectives or work performance and the coordinating agency should try to contain this. It is expected that the gaining awareness to solve the problems of rural poor could be momentarily strengthened by a sectoral approach at the micro-level and area approach at the macro-level. Each sector—primary, secondary and tertiary has to develop so as to absorb the requisite priorities to strengthen the productivity-employment conflict. According to a recent evaluation, much attention has to be given to the development of secondary and tertiary sectors in the rural system so as to contain the population exodus to unproductive systems. Each region—backward, developing and developed has to grow within the specific sector or across so as to bring in a balanced technological base for development.

Sectoral Growth and Rural Development

The performance of rural development programmes has been similar to that of Indian planning in that both are poised with many take-off problems. Given limited resources and ambitious goals, it should be paramount that the desirable goals are achieved quickly and steadily. The performance has been one of slow growth and sectoral disparities. The problem of poverty alleviation both in absolute and relative terms lingers there on defying many solutions.

Agriculture is the predominant primary sector where the bulk of the employment is utilised. At 1970-71 prices, the national per capita income during 1985-86 has been Rs 786, whereas in agriculture it was only Rs 425. About 45 per cent of rural population and 25 per cent of urban population is estimated to be under the poverty line which has been fixed at Rs 107 per month per capita for rural areas and at Rs 123 for urban population. The low productivity in agricultural sector demands diversion of agricultural labour to non-farm activities in the rural sector itself and also to industry and trade in urban areas.

The number of agricultural labourers is about 56 million (constituting about 25 per cent of the total workers). Farmers having less than 2 ha. of land holding constitute about 75 per cent, their share in area being only 20 per cent. Given that the area under irrigation is only 30 per cent and area prone to drought and floods is more than 260 million ha. the plight of rural poor assumes gravity.

Many rural programmes have had emphasised more on the subsidy elements and short-term abatements. The excessive importance given to the primary sector and the resulting ineffectual impact are eye-openers for restructuring the entire programme. In the rural system apart from agriculture, many other sub-sectors have experienced mixed growth patterns and structural changes in the recent past. Rural reconstruction can take place only when the basic infrastructural facilities and absorptive capacity is institutionalised. Rural development should be viewed as a process of technical change and dealt with accordingly. The new agricultural technology could succeed in many areas only because of the favourable absorptive capacity expressed in terms of adaptability of new techniques.

Agriculture policy may indicate a direction toward special programmes so as to stimulate various development processes. The growth of different sub-sectors through market-oriented incentives (infrastructural, institutional, financial, etc.) should be viewed from the long-term prospective rather than as short-term relief subsidies. The question is whether the concerned programmes initiate a favourable impact on the growth process. Giving subsidy to major sectors like agriculture may not be productive any longer and this calls for substitution by above mentioned incentives which would bring in the desired effect. The larger the quantum of incentive components in the programmes, the larger the income increase would be for the beneficiaries. And the incentives have to be tailored according to the specific objectives, area priority and approach of the programme.

A case can be made out to see whether the effort of spreading the impact of limited resources on a very wide area could be productive to the desired intensity. A possible alternate solution could be to identify problem areas and sectors and initiate a process wherein a system similar to international division of labour could be ushered in. If a particular area is specialised in particular activities, the same could be developed by providing special incentives through specialised agencies. Division of labour should be not only in respect of apportioning programmes to the selected areas but also in the matter of implementation and follow-up action by the specialised agencies.

After agriculture, labour concentration in rural areas is marked in khadi and village industries, handloom, bidi rolling, etc. Special programmes aimed at developing the subsidiary occupations of agricultural labourers would go a long way in achieving the objective of growth with stability. The concentration of specific programmes for specific areas would not only improve the production structure but also employment potentiality.

We may consider the case of bidi-rolling which is a major rural activity only after crop cultivation. Development of this particular activity will not only improve the status of rural poor in specific areas, but also influence inter linkages between other areas and sectors. The rate of adoption of any improved package denotes the level of local participation. Rural programmes should not only look after short term priorities but also take to consideration in inter play of different sub-sectors toward a system of long-run growth orientation. Normally, it is found that multi-activity labourers are better off than say, single-activity labourers like agriculture workers. The programmes, therefore, should have a base wherein the single-activity priorities are transformed into multiple-activities. The multi-activity enterprises, consequent on assistance, should work toward this direction. It should be evident that development of rural sector is too complex and would demand huge structural improvements.

An attempt has been made to evaluate the contribution of a specific sub-sector like bidi-rolling toward rural development, covering aspects like labour absorption, working conditions, income generation and living conditions of the workers and so on.

Though bidi smoking could be termed as an unhealthy habit growing of tobacco (similar to moriculture or pulp trees) has to be encouraged so that the population dependant on that could survive. It is estimated that about 80 per cent of all male and 40 per cent of all female use tobacco in one form or the other in our country. An average Indian consumes about 700 gms tobacco per year, of which about 43 per cent is in the form of bidis. Bidi-rolling provides employment of about 4 million full-time and part-time rural workers. The annual turnover by the bidi industries is over Rs 1,500 crores. A study of such a major sub-sector in the rural system would highlight the specific problems faced by that sector as well as its contribution to the upliftment of those for whom development needs are predominant.

REFERENCES

Anon, *The Study of Implementation of IRDP*, NABARD, Bombay, 1984.

M.L. Dantwala, et al. (ed.), *Asian Seminar on Rural Development: The Indian Experience*, Oxford and IBH Pub. Co., New Dehli, 1986.

M.L. Dantwala and J.N. Barmeda 'Rural Development: Approaches and Issues' in M L. Dantwala and others (ed.), *Indian Agricultural Development Since Independence*, Oxford and IBH Pub. Co., New Delhi, 1916.

D.R D.S. 'Six Monthly Seminar on IRDP', D.R.D.S, Mangalore, 1986.

R.P. Misra (ed.), Rural Development: *Capitalist and Socialist Paths, Vol I: An Overview* Concept Pub. Co, New Delhi, 1985.

V.S. Mahajan (ed.), *Studies in Indian Agriculture and Rural Development*, Deep and Deep Pub. Co, New Delhi, 1986.

Programme Evaluation Organisation, *Evaluation Report on Integrated Rural Development Programme*, Planning Commission, New Delhi, 1985.

2

BIDI INDUSTRY

Introduction

In tobacco, leaf is the major item of consumption. Tobacco is smoked in the form of cigarettes, cigars, cheroots, bidis, pipe and hookah. Surti, zarda, qiwam, quid, etc. are some of the forms in which it is chewed. It is also inhaled in the form of snuff. The same type of tobacco cannot be used for all the purposes. For different uses, different types of tobacco are grown in varying soil and agro-climatic conditions. Tobacco wastes are used for industrial purposes.

Cigarette is the chief form in which tobacco is consumed in the world. During 1983, an estimated quantity of over 4,56,303 crore pieces were produced. United States (66,700 crore pieces), Peoples' Republic of China (96,260 crore pieces) and Japan (30,550 crore pieces) are the major cigarette producers in the world. India produced 8,500 crore pieces in that year (about 1.9 per cent of world total). The major exporters are Bulgaria, Federal Republic of Germany, Netherlands, United Kingdom and the United States. These countries put together, exported over 75 per cent of world's total cigarette export of 34,875 crore pieces during 1983. India exported about 160 crore pieces, much less than the previous year record of 500 crore pieces.

Bidi tobacco ranks second in the country next only to flue-cured virginia tobacco in area and accounts for the highest share (37.3 per cent) of total tobacco production. In Karnataka, bidi tobacco accounts for about 65 per cent of total tobacco area. It is grown largely in Chikodi, Hukkeri and Gokak taluks of Belgaum district and also in Bellary district. The area in

Mysore district has declined in recent years. Bidi tobacco produced in Karnataka is famous for its quality. Good quality bidi tobacco is grown in medium black or red soils. Top quality tobacco, however, is grown in the deep black soils along the Krishna river and its tributaries. Necessary crop cultivation practices, rotation, fertilisation, and proper plant protection measures, besides healthy curing of the tobacco leaves, improve the quality. Due to improper processing or storage, the quality of tobacco may be affected. If poor quality or under-processed tobacco supplied along with similar quality of tendu leaves, quality difference and wastage become quite substantial.

The price per quintal of Gujarat bidi tobacco in Mangalore during the later half of 1984 has been Rs 950 to Rs 1500 and for the Nippani type, the price ranged between Rs 1000 to Rs 1600. Currently, the price has increased to over Rs 1200 to Rs 1800 per quintal. Bidi export during 1983-84 was 867 million tonnes valued at Rs 4.2 crore. During 1982-83, the exported quantity was 332 million tonnes only. The export of bidi tobacco as a proportion to total production is about 3.5 per cent, while for the entire tobacco industry, the proportion is 25 per cent. This is because of export of sizeable quantity of cigarettes. Though bidi exports formed only about 0.8 per cent of total tobacco exports (both manufactured and unmanufactured) in recent years, a larger quantity of bidis, especially to the Gulf countries, is increasingly being exported.

Bidi Manufacturing

The bidi industry is wide-spread in our country. Bidi manufacturing is not uniform in terms of capital invested, number of persons employed, the size of bidi and also in terms of concentration. There are a few units in the organised sector, but most of the units are in the unorganised cottage sector. The industry is not run with the help of power or machineries. No fixed premises are required unless it is other than "home-working". The only tools that are required for the bidi manufacturing are a pair of scissors for cutting the wrapper, a small hand-knife and trays to keep raw materials. The process is simple but does require much skill for a neat and even turnout.

Bidi tobacco and tendu leaves are the main raw materials

used in bidi manufacturing. The other materials used are cotton thread, maida for glue making and coal used in batti and packing material.

The manufacturing process consists of rolling, sorting, drying, labelling and packing. Before rolling, the wrapper leaves are soaked in water overnight and then cut into suitable sizes for wrapping the blended tobacco mix. The size of the leaves, the nature of tobacco blend will vary according to different trade-marks. The procedure for rolling consists in taking a small quantity of tobacco flakes on the wrapper kept ready for the purpose, spreading the flakes evenly and then rolling the wrapper between fingers diagonally to give a conical shape. A piece of cotton is tied toward the smoking end. The edges of the wrapper pieces are placed partially inside this end and the flattened smoking tip remains partly open. The broad end is closed by folding the open edges inward. The size of the bidi may be 5.0 cm, 6.25 cm, or 7.5 cm. in length according to different manufacturing practices. An average roller can roll two to three bidis per minute though some experienced hands can roll even five to six bidis. When the rolling process is over, the bidis are packed in bundles of 25 and then bigger bundles and brought to the employers or contractors.

Bidi industry is organised in three different stages. First is the factory stage where the manufacturer is the owner of the factory. Under the contract system of employment, which is most prevalent, the trade-mark owner supplies bidi tobacco and leaves to the contractor, who on receiving the materials, manufactures bidis by directly employing labourers or by distributing the raw materials among home-workers. The latter form of arrangement is quite common wherein it is women who primarily roll bidis with the assistance of a small proportion of male members and children.

In a few cases, the workers may get the raw materials directly from the manufacturers and supply the bidis directly to them. In some cases, it is not uncommon to find bidi manufacturing being undertaken in very small scales. A family may roll out and sell few thousands per day. Moreover, up to a certain limit of production, small scale bidi manufacturing is kept out of the excise purview by the government, which encourages small scale production.

Production Estimates

India occupies the second place in the world in respect of area under tobacco though it ranks third after China and United States in respect of production. The per hectare yield of tobacco was about 990 kgs/ha. in 1977-78 while the world average was 1295 kgs/ha. Table 2.1 presents estimates of area, production

Table 2.1 : Estimates of Area, Production and Yield of Tobacco in Important States

State	1980-81			1983-84		
	Area ('000 ha.)	*Production* ('000 mt)	*Yield (kgs)*	*Area* ('000 ha.)	*Praduction* ('000 mt)	*Yield (kgs)*
Andhra Pradesh	169.4	164.0	968	187.1	191 0	1026
Bihar	12.5	10.0	800	13.4	13.4	1000
Gujarat	121.5	185.2	1524	108.0	186.9	1725
Karnataka	51.6	33 9	657	480 0	28 8	600
Maharashtra	11.9	6 8	571	10.1	7.9	782
Orissa	21.1	11.3	536	18.7	10.2	545
Tamil Nadu	14.5	22.4	1545	12.4	13.7	1105
Uttar Pradesh	15.4	20.2	1312	14.7	19.7	1340
West Bengal	19.0	17.4	916	15.1	15.5	1026
Total for the above States	436.9	471.2	1078	427.8	488.0	1141

Source: *Indian Tobacco Journal*, various issues.

and yield of tobacco in important states during 1980-81 and 1983-84. Total tobacco area in the major producing states stood at 0.44 million hectare during 1980-81 and slightly declined to 0.43 million hectare during 1983-84. But production increased from 0.47 million metric tonne to 0.49 million metric tonne during this period, increasing the per hectare yield level from 1078 to 1141 kgs. Among the states, Andhra Pradesh and

Gujarat accounted for the bulk of the area and production shares. Karnataka followed next, but the yield rate has been below the national average. Gujarat, Uttar Pradesh and Tamil Nadu reported high productivity figures.

Bidi as a form of smoke is believed to have originated during the 19th century in Madhya Pradesh, spreading to other areas. The cultivation of bidi tobacco is concentrated in Charotar area of Gujarat, Nippani area in Karnataka and Kohlapur and Sangli districts in Maharashtra. Gujarat, Karnataka and Maharashtra are major bidi producers. The total area under bidi tobacco during 1977-78 was about 1.1 lakh hectare and production of bidi tobacco was 1.6 lakh metric tonne. This shows that when compared to the average tobacco yield, bidi tobacco productivity is at least 50 per cent higher than that. During 1973-74, about 71.6 million tonne of bidis were exported at a value of Rs 1.5 million. During 1977-78, the quantity exported increased to 286 million tonne at a value of Rs 8.7 million. During the previous year, export of bidis constituted only about 0.2 per cent of total tobacco export. During 1977-78, the proportion increased to about 0.8 per cent. The excise revenues from tobacco products reached over Rs 465 crores in 1977-78 from Rs. 37.5 crores in 1964-65. During 1983-84, the central excise revenue was about Rs 1070 crores and bidi share in this was 12.2 per cent. When compared to 1982-83, there has been a decline of over 2.0 per cent in the share of bidi to the excise revenue.

The annual collection of bidi leaves is estimated to exceed 0.3 million metric tonnes of which nearly 50 per cent share is accounted for by Madhya Pradesh. Orissa, Maharashtra and Andhra Pradesh are the other major producers, accounting for about 30 to 50 thousand metric tonne each. Bidi leaf trade has been brought under the control of the respective state governments owing to its economic importance. Substantial quantity of bidi leaves is also being exported to some of the neighbouring countries. Total quantity exported during 1981-82 had been about 4254 million tonne, fetching a value of Rs 3 crore.

During 1976-77, about 1.3 lakh metric tonne of bidi tobacco and about 4 lakhs metric tonne of bidi leaves were used to manufacture an estimated quantity of 52,000 crore pieces. The current production is estimated of about 1,00,000 crore pieces per annum. Madhya Pradesh is the leading bidi producer, followed by Gujarat and Karnataka.

The increase in the consumption of bidi tobacco has been modest at 1.2 per cent per annum in the mid seventies. During 1960-61 to 1964-65 bidi tobacco demand growth was at 2.5 per cent (similar to population growth); during 1965-66 to 1974-75, the demand registered a modest increase at 1.0 per cent per annum. In the years 1975-76 and 1976-77, the growth was impressive at over 25 per cent when compared to the preceding years. No satisfactory explanation has been provided for this, except that strict excise vigilence enabled reporting of a higher figure. According to NCAER projections, the internal demand for bidi tobacco was 1.34 lakh metric tonne in 1977-78. The bidi demand in the eighties will not be more than this quantity. The reason for holding this view was due to the fact that during the three years preceding to 1977-78, the consumption figures were quite high. But the Expert Group's Report on Tobacco projected over 1.52 lakh tonnes of bidi tobacco consumption during 1985-86. The per capita consumption of bidi tobacco, which stood at 184 gms in 1975-76 increased to 221 gms in the succeeding year owing to high reporting. The per capita consumption has stagnated at that level ever since.

Cost of Production

As the industry is essentially in the unorganised sector, no source is able to furnish reliable cost details. Since different manufacturers choose different practices, production scales, wage rates, etc. it is difficult to arrive at uniform cost structure. The Expert Group study has compared the cost structure of bidi manufacturing as conducted by the Institute of the Public Enterprises, All India Bidi Industry Federation and Annual Survey of Industries. Table 2.2 describes the comparaitive cost structure as reported by the Expert Group. According to IPE (Institute of Public Enterprise) survey results, the cost of manufacturing 1000 bidis was Rs 16.31 in 1976-77. Raw materials shared 35.6 per cent of this, salaries and wages 37.4 per cent and excise duty 21.8 per cent. Estimates from the same Institute revealed that the share of raw materials, salaries and wages, and excise duty was in the order of 33.3, 43.5, and 23.2 per cent respectively in another study. The All India Bidi Industry

Table 2.2 : Comparative Cost Structure of Bidi

(Rs per 1000 bidis)

Cost Element	*IPE Survey Results*	*Bidi Fed Estimates*	*IPE Estimates*
Tobacco	2 32	2.20	1.79
Bidi leaves	2.23	2.50	2.12
Packing material	0 76	—	0.52
Other expenses	1.34	1.00	0.74
Salaries and wages	6.10	6.00	6.75
Excise duty on tobacco	—	0.84	—
Excise duty on bidis	3 56	2.00	3.60
Total	16.31	14.54	15.52

Source: *Report on Tobacco*, Expert Group, Ministry of Commerce and Civil Supplies, New Delhi, 1978, p. 204.

Federation estimates showed that the proportion of the above three cost elements was 32.3, 41.3 and 12.5 per cent respectively in cost of production.

The raw material cost includes bidi tobacco, bidi leaves and packing material. The share of tobacco and leaves has been of the same level in most of the cases referred to above.

According to IPE report, the cost of production of 1000 bidis made by self-employed bidi rollers was Rs 3.01 (this includes only bidi tobacco, leaf and other expenses) in Madhya Pradesh (being the lowest), and Rs 3.26 in Tamil Nadu (being the highest). Wages for rolling is the biggest element in the cost structure, forming 35 per cent in Orissa and 54 per cent in Kerala of the total cost. The Excise duty ranges from 20 per cent in Kerala to 26.5 per cent in Orissa. Cost of bidi leaf ranges from 8.9 to 17.4 per cent. The contribution of bidi tobacco varies from 9.7 to 14 per cent excluding Kerala where flue-cured virginia tobacco is also used. These particulars are with respect to large and medium scale units. For the small scale units, the wage for rolling varies from 37 per cent in Orissa to 58 per cent in Kerala. Excise duty share ranges from 20.7 per cent in Kerala to 28.4 per cent in Orissa. The share of bidi leaf ranges between 9.4 per cent in Kerala and 18.4 in Orissa and that of bidi tobacco from 11.33 per cent in Kerala to 15.3 per cent in Orissa. For unbranded bidis, which do not bear central excise duty, the cost structure indicates that wages for rolling share the maximum proportion (50.2 per cent in Orissa and 75.4 per cent in Kerala). Table 2.3 describes the

Table 2.3 ; Cost Structure Ranking in Units

Sector	*Cost Elements*			
	Wages	*Excise*	*Leaves*	*Tobacco*
Large and medium units —rank	1	2	3	4
%	35—54	20—27	9—17	10—14
Small scale (branded bidis) — rank	1	2	3	4
%	37—58	21—28	9—18	11—15
Small scale (unbranded) —rank	1	4	2	3
%	44—68	11—15	11—22	14—18
Small scale (unbranded and non-excisable) —rank	1	—	2	3
%	50—75	—	12—25	15—21

Source: *Report on Tobacco*, p. 213.

ranking of different cost elements in the large and medium scale and small scale units. First is wages, followed by excise duty, leaves and tobacco for branded bidis. For nonbranded bidis, the share of excise duty was nil.

The Expert Group furnishes the cost structure of bidi manufacturing in Karnataka during 1976-77 (Table 2.4), in which it notes that under ideal conditions the contribution of wages is about 33.6 per cent, followed by other manufacturing expenses (23.6 per cent), excise duty (17.5 per cent), tobacco (10.1 per cent), retailers' margin (9.7 per cent), manufacturers' margin

Table 2.4 : Cost Structure of 3" Branded Bidi in Karnataka

(Rs per 1000 bidis)

Cost Element	*Under Ideal Conditions*		*Assuming Certain Malpractices*	
	Rs	*%*	*Rs*	*%*
Tobacco	2.07	10.08	1.76	8.57
Margin of commission agent	0.10	0.49	0.41	2.00
Wages and benefits (20%)	6.90	33.59	4.00	19.47
Leaves and other expenses	4.84	23.56	4.84	23.56
Excise duty	3 60	17.53	3.60	17.53
Manufacturer's margin	0.53	2.58	3.43	16.70
Wholesaler's margin	0.50	2.43	0.50	2.43
Retailer's margin	2.00	9.74	2.00	9.74
Total	20.54	100.00	20 54	100.00

Source: *Report on Tobacco*, p. 217.

(2.6 per cent), whole-salers' margin (2.4 per cent) and margin of commission agents (0.5 per cent) If certain malpractices are assumed, it is seen that the contribution of wages declines to 19.5 per cent whereas, that of manufacturers' margin increases to 16.7 per cent and that of margin to commission agents to 2 per cent. It is seen that the manufacturers do follow some exploitative measures which deprive the bidi-rollers of their due share. This explains for the growing awareness and unionisation amongst bidi-rollers in recent times for better wage structure and other benefits.

The contribution of labour charges in manufacture of bidi has remained to 35 to 40 per cent in most of the states since long.

Some of the problems faced in bidi industry have been competition from cheap cigarettes, difference in wage rates across the states, unionisation levels, existence of duplicate brands and less effectiveness of cooperative workers societies. The tendu leaves grow only in certain places like in Madhya Pradesh forests and have to be transported during the monsoon season itself when they are fresh. Transportation by rail wagons and storage and quality maintenance are some of the limitations faced in this. As regards tobacco, improper processing sometimes harms the flakes, as a result of which the quality of bidi is affected. Improper storage during the rainy season also affects the quality of both tobacco and leaves.

Since bidi industry is unorganised, there exists a panorama of manufacturing systems. There are family units as well as very big units employing thousands of bidi-rollers. Not only that, there are branded and unbranded bidis. There exists a sizeable proportion of duplicate brands also. By the latter method, not only the excise duty due to the government is avoided, but the rollers are also unduly exploited by low wage rates and the consumers victimised by low quality and spurious products. In some places, duplicate account as big as 25 per cent of total bidi sales. Apart from this, the bidi industry faces competition from cheap machine-made cigarettes. With one kg of tobacco, 4 to 5 times less of cigarettes are machine-rolled when compared to hand-rolled bidi. Cigarette industry as such is thoroughly mechanised and large-scaled. The cigarette manufacturers with a view to capturing the market of low income groups, normally fix low prices for some common brands of cigarettes, compensating the loss, if any, by increasing the prices of superior brands. The changing life styles compel the low income consumers to prefer cheap cigarettes to bidis even in rural areas. Tobacco and bidi prices have increased tremendously over these years, owing to steep rise in excise duty and other expenses. As a result of which, the demand for bidis (and also other tobacco products) has not shown any appreciable increase.

The wage rates for bidi-rolling vary from state to state. In some states where there is proximity to tendu leaves like Madhya Pradesh and Orissa, the wage rates are lower when compared to states like Kerala and Karnataka. These locational factors coupled with cheap labour have necessitated lower bidi prices in the southern states which have to face competition from them. Moreover, the intensity of unionisation in states like

Kerala and Karnataka have been responsible for comparatively high wage rates and increased cost of production.

REFERENCES

Directorate of Marketing and Inspection, *Marketing of Bidi Tobacco, Tendu Leaf and Bidis in India*, Ministry of Food, Agriculture, Community Development and Cooperation, Nagpur, 1967.

All India Bidi Industry Federation, *Memorandum*, Bombay, 1967.

Expert Group, *Report on Tabacco*, Ministry of Commerce and Supplies, New Delhi, 1979.

All India Bidi Industry Federation, *Bidi Bulletin*, various issues.

Indian Tobacco Journal, various issues.

3

PROBLEM AND METHOD

Labour Utilisation in Rural Sector

Labour workforce in rural sector constitutes about 67 per cent of total workforce in the country and it has taken over 20 years to reach this from a base proportion of 75 per cent. According to neo-classical theory, where market conditions are assumed to be perfect, labour allocation is optimal and labour resources are fully employed. If any disequilibrium results from this state of affairs government has to intervene. The trigger policies may aim at either influencing the effective demand for food or that of labour. The increase in effective demand for food would induce increased supply of food, thereby increasing employment of labour in crop cultivation.

As regards influences on the effective demand for labour, the so-called rural development programmes adopted by the government in the recent years attempt at increased employment of labour, especially in off-peak seasons. Employment guarantee, provision of minimum wages, effective union participation (the current level is only about 1.0 per cent according to Rural Labour Enquiry Committee, 1975), etc. may improve the effective demand.

In rural areas, cultivators constitute about 51 per cent of total workers and agricultural labour about 30 per cent. When compared to the 1971 census, the above figures of 1981 census show that there has been an increase of over 15 per cent in agriculture labour class over the decade.

Of late, various government programmes as well as market forces have influenced a certain degree of diversification in rural activities. Cultivation of commercial crops, commercialisation of subsistence crops, livestock enterprises, new energy programmes, rural industrialisation, etc. are some of the factors in increasing demand for more and better utilisation of labour.

The conditions of labour vary from industry to industry and within industry. The conditions remain exploitative in the feudal set-up with little bargaining power for labour. Several studies have been done on the conditions of agriculture labour especially on those belonging to the weaker sections. Nowadays, better labour participation, organisation of different categories of labour, participation in the decision making process, etc. have initiated a movement toward a fair treatment to rural labour. However, it may be said that when industrial labour itself is not thoroughly emancipated, the conditions of rural labour still remain in a deplorable condition.

Productivity in the agricultural sector has been low when compared to other sectors, indicating low technology level and under-utilisation of labour. Under-utilisation of labour manifests into low productivity and thereby deficient effective demand, thus increasing the problem of food supply and nutrition. The recent Indian experience has shown that labour migration to other sectors has been negligible and under-productive. Yet agriculture sector has to fulfil the objectives of increased supply of food, export and better linkage with other sectors.

To utilise the under-utilised rural labour in a better way becomes a crucial issue for increased supply conditions—both food and employment. Modern agricultural technology, improvement in irrigation infrastructure, etc. have considerably helped in this direction. Emphasizing on supplementary sources of job opportunities greatly relieves the pressure on land and also improves the status of agricultural labour. Founding of many agro-industries further strengthens the technology base of the rural sector.

Dairying, cash crop cultivation, cottage industries, etc. attempt to effect better utilisation of labour in the agricultural sector. Bidi-rolling in the specific areas fulfils similar objective in differing degrees according to the demand for bidi and supply of rural labour for the purpose. No doubt, because of high labour requirements in bidi-rolling, crop cultivation may be converted into less labour intensive or high labour intensive crops may be no longer cultivated in large areas.

The present study attempts to study the labour conditions as falling between the urbanised and the unorganised strata. Bidi-rolling labour suits exactly this premise, wherein active unionisation co-exists side by side with un-unionised labour. As a matter of fact, bidi-rolling does not come strictly under the industrial purview.

It is estimated that there are over 4.3 million full-time and part-time labourers engaged in bidi manufacturing. That would seem that besides agriculture, bidi-making is the next major activity in the rural areas. Of the total bidi labour, a sizeable portion belongs to rural small cultivating and labour classes. Another peculiar feature is that over 75 per cent of bidi-rollers are women and children.

Objectives

The study has the objectives of attempting to evaluate labour absorption in bidi-rolling with respect to occupation, locality and method of manufacturing hookup. Since women form the major labour force, the study aims at evaluating their contribution to rural development; and how woman and child labour are being utilised, and the nature of complementary, supplementary or substituting occupations. It would be profitable to study labour participation in bidi-rolling and to see whether their lifestyle is different from others.

The specific objectives of the study are :

(i) To find out the contribution of full-time versus part-time bidi-rolling labour;

(ii) To study the differences between rural and semi-urban situations;

(iii) To find out the contribution of man, woman and child labour to employment, production, etc.

(iv) To find out whether bidi labour requires IRDP assistance, and

(v) To see if cooperative rolling could become profitable and at the same time less exploitative in the system.

Various aspects of the conditions of the bidi labourers like pattern of employment, differences in income levels and the above according to different seasons are important issues to be discussed. Nutrition, health, education, and active participation are other factors which are to be evaluated. The income, expenditure, and saving patterns among different types of bidi-rollers and in different set-ups should be indicative of nature of assistance they demand off—for example, from IRDP, co-operation and the like. With this, it is hoped to evaluate life styles of different categories of bidi-rollers and other activities of the workers, thus bringing out the contribution of bidi industry to the rural economy.

The Method

Of the 4 million bidi labourers in the country, about 12 per cent of this is accounted for by Karnataka. Dakshina Kannada district is the major bidi producing centre in the state and one of the concentrated bidi producing places in the country. There are over 22 principal employers and total number of establishments including the contractors is about 3760 in mid 1985. Total number of bidi workers registered as per the Bidi and Cigar Act is about 2.68 lakhs. Of this, 80 per cent are home-workers and the rest are employed in establishments. The system followed is the contract system of employment. The principal employers supply the raw materials to the contractors or subcontractors and these in turn engage labourers and supply the finished product to the principal employers. The contractors have to maintain the particulars about the registered labour and they will have to report to the principal employers about the quantum of output produced by them. The principal employers or manufacturers settle the wage bill and the other benefits like provident fund contribution, bonus, dearness allowance, holiday allowance and maternity allowance. Besides these, the children of bidi workers get scholarships for study and the Bidi Workers Welfare Fund is being utilised for the benefit of the labour class.

For the method to select the sample areas of the study, the specific problems of bidi-rollers have been kept in due consideration. A semi-urban area (Ullal town) has been selected in Mangalore taluk where bidi-rolling is concentrated. Being close to the Mangalore city and having a population of 25,000, the area is having diversified activities. Over 25 per cent of the total population are dependent on bidi manufacturing. The other occupations found common are fisheries, agriculture, tile making, automobile repairing, etc.

In this town, 52 bidi-rolling families were selected for study, showing differing groups of part-time and full-time calling The employment, income, and expenditure patterns were considered for the entire family and the families were grouped according to the share of bidi income to total income.

The rural sample has been selected in Bantwal taluk (Pajir). This village has a population of over 4,400. Of the total 700 households, about 50 per cent depends partly or fully on bidi manufacturing. 44 households were selected in the village for study. The reference period related to June 1984 to May 1985 season. Some of the basic statistics pertaining to the sample villages are presented in Table 3.1.

Table 3.1 : Some Basic Statistics

Particulars	*Unit*	*Ullal*	*Pajir*
Total area	ha.	780.2	1,296.9
Area under cultivation	ha.	236.0	392.1
Area under paddy	ha.	125 5	336 7
Area under garden	ha.	200.5	55.4
Total population			
(1981 census)	Male	12,921	2,297
	Eemale	12,587	2,121
	Total	25,508	4,418
Total households		4,000	700
Households, depending on bidi-rolling		1,000	350
No. of bidi contractors		25	10

The analysis pertained to classification of part-time and ful-time bidi families, calculating season-wise male, female, and child labour utilisation in bidi and other occupations. The first season refers to monsoon months June to September, the second season, September to December and the third, February to May. Bidi productivity, income from bidi as well as other occupations have been computed to evaluate bidi productivity in relation to other occupations. The consumption expenditure pattern across different household groups would indicate the nature of food, health, education fuel and other items of expenditure in predominantly bidi families as contrasted to others. The analysis would also consider particulars like unionisation and other general information.

An attempt is also made to evaluate the performance of female-headed vs. male-headed bidi households with respect to certain variables. It is understood that bidi-rolling being an important sector in the process of rural development, a study of the same would not only try to highlight its role but also emphasize its right perspective in the process.

REFERENCES

P.K. Bardhan et at., *Labour Absorption in Indian Agriculture: Some Exploratory Investigations*, ILO—ARTEP, Bangkok, 1978.

A. Booth and R.M. Sundrum, *Labour Absorption in Agriculture*, Oxford University Press, New Delhi, 1984.

4

EMPLOYMENT AND INCOME STRUCTURE

The Group Classification

The samples have been grouped according to income levels. This is to differentiate contribution of bidi-rolling to total income of the household. It could be surmised that if the household obtains over half of the total income by an occupation, that particular occupation becomes the major source of livelihood. In the case of bidi-rolling also, it should be possible to have a demarcation between full-time and part-time engagement.

However, it was not possible to get a high degree of relevant information, from some samples taking a 50 per cent demarcation. They might not contribute toward bidi-rolling as the principal occupation of the sample household. Owing to non-reporting and other factors, bidi-rolling has been treated as the principal occupation considering a 60 per cent break-even point. This would suggest that households reporting total income as obtainable from bidi-rolling to the extent of 60 per cent and higher can be termed as full-time bidi-rolling households. Here, it should be noted that definitions of full-time occupation vary according to different sources. In some cases, a 75 per cent break-even point is considered as an index of whole-time occupation.

Based on the different income levels in two samples, the households have been divided into eight groups. The first four groups are part-time households. In Ullal, a semi-urban town, it is found that about 41 per cent of the part-time bidi-rolling households report income from bidi-rolling as a low proportion of total household income. The first group has less than 30 per cent of the total income accruable by bidi-rolling but accounts for over 41 per cent of the part-time samples. The second group (bidi income contributing between 30 to 40 per cent of total income) accounts for about one third. The other two groups (40 to 50 per cent and 50 to 60 per cent) account for the balance.

In the first group (34 households), contribution in income from bidi-rolling is 18.8 per cent to total income. The respective shares in other groups are 33.4 per cent, 46.3 per cent, and 51.7 per cent to total income. It is seen that in the part-time bidi-rolling households, about 30 per cent of total income is obtained by bidi-rolling.

The full-time bidi-rolling households (18) report 60 to 100 per cent bidi income to total income. Taken individually, the households which depend only on bidi-rolling account for over 45 per cent in these groups. There are four groups—60 to 70 per cent, 70 to 80 per cent, 80 to 90 per cent, and 90 to 100 per cent falling under this category. The average contribution of bidi to total income is 60 per cent in the fifth group. It is 70.7 per cent, 81.4 per cent and 100 per cent respectively in the succeeding size groups. About 82 per cent of total income is contributed by bidi-rolling in this category. The average contribution of bidi to total income for the entire Ullal sample is about 43 per cent.

As contrast to this semi-urban sample, the rural sample of Pajir reports about 60 per cent of total income as contributed by bidi-rolling for the entire sample. This shows that bidi-rolling activity is more pronounced in rural areas of the district. In Ullal, the major activities are fishing, tile-making and agriculture, whereas in Pajir, only agriculture is the major occupation. In the Pajir sample, the part-time households number 17, where contribution of bidi to total income is about 40 per cent. The full-time bidi households numbering 27, report over 75 per cent contribution by bidi-rolling to total income. When compared to the semi-urban sample, the higher contribution of bidi to total income in Pajir suggests that, in the former, the choice between the occupations is not that much restricted as in the latter.

Family Members and Workers

Tables 4.1 and 4.2 present the total number of family members and workers in Ullal and Pajir according to the income size groups. As a small proportion child labour is utilised in bidi-rolling, that labour is also included besides male and female labourers. In other occupations, only male and female workers are utilised. For the sake of calculation, one female worker is treated at par with a male worker and two child workers have been considered equal to one adult worker.

Table 4 3 describes the percentage of male, female and child workers to total sample population in the two areas. As regards female workers, the percentage of bidi workers to total population is also considered because of their high contribution to work. In the part-time households, the proportion of male members employed constitutes about 74 per cent of their population in Ullal. About 83.3 per cent of the female population is employed in different occupations. The proportion of female population engaged in bidi-rolling is about 73.6 per cent, i.e. about 88.0 per cent of the employed female workers. As regards child ladour, 1.2 per cent is engaged in employment and that too in bidi-rolling only. In Pajir, the proportion of working population is higher for male and child workers and slightly less for female workers.

In the full-time households, a lower proportion of males are employed but slightly higher proportion of male and child population are employed in bidi-rolling and all occupations put together. The proportion is very low among male population in Pajir, but there, a higher proportion of females and children are employed. It is seen that 82.1 per cent and 58.8 per cent of male population has been employed in Ullal and Pajir respectively. The proportion for females is 84.0 per cent and 91.0 per cent and for children 3.5 per cent and 15.4 per cent respectively. About 76.4 per cent of total females are engaged in bidi-rolling in Ullal and in Pajir, the proportion is 77.7 per cent showing not much difference in female employment. Of the total bidi workers, females constitute over 85 per cent in Ullal and 87 per cent in Pajir, showing a similar picture for both the places.

Table 4.1 : Family Members and Workers in Ullal

Size Group	*H.H No*	*Bidi Workers*				*Other Workers*				*Total Family Members*				*Standard Consumption Units*
		Ml	*Fl*	*Ch*	*Total*	*Ml*	*Fl*	*Ch*	*Total*	*Ml*	*Fl*	*Ch*	*Total*	
30%	14	--	19	--	19	26	3	—	29	35	30	25	90	77.0
30—40	11	3	18	1	21.5	16	2	–	18	26	23	36	85	68.3
40 -50	5	—	7	—	7	5	—	—	5	7	8	13	28	22.0
50—60	4	—	9	—	9	4	1	—	5	5	11	6	22	18.5
Sub-total	34	3	53	1	56 5	51	6	—	57	73	72	80	225	185.8
60—70	5	1	10	—	11	4	—	—	4	5	11	8	24	19.7
70—80	3	—	6	1	6.5	3	—	—	3	4	7	7	18	14.5

80—90	2	1	3	2	5	1	—	—	1	5	4	8	17	13.4
90—100	8	7	9	—	16	—	—	—	—	10	12	11	33	27.4
Sub-total	18	9	28	3	38.5	8	—	—	8	24	34	34	92	75.0
Total	52	12	81	4	95	59	6	—	63	97	106	114	317	260.8

Table 4.2 : Family Members and Workers in Pajir

Size Group	H.H. No.	Bidi Workers				Other Workers				Total Family Members				Standard Consumption Units
		Ml	Fl	Ch	Total	Ml	Fl	Ch	Total	Ml	Fl	Ch	Total	
I	4	—	6	—	6	5	3	—	8	6	11	10	27	21.9
II	6	—	8	2	9	11	—	—	11	12	8	15	35	28.1
III	2	—	4	—	4	3	2	—	5	4	6	2	12	10.6
IV	15	1	11	2	13	5	2	—	7	8	15	6	29	25.1
Sub-total	17	1	29	4	32	24	7	—	31	30	40	33	103	85.8
V	11	2	24	2	27	11	3	—	14	22	27	15	64	55.3
VI	4	1	7	3	9.5	2	2	—	4	6	12	6	24	20.4

VII	2	—	6	—	6	3	1	—	4	5	7	3	15	13.1
VIII	10	3	21	3	25.5	—	2	—	2	17	26	21	64	53.6
Sub-total	27	6	58	8	68	16	8	—	24	50	72	45	167	141.8
Total	44	7	87	12	100	40	15	—	55	80	112	78	270	227.6

Table 4.3 : Percentage of Workers to Total Sample Population

Size Group	ULLAL Male	ULLAL Female %age to Total	ULLAL Female %age of Bidi Workers	ULLAL Child	PAJIR Male	PAJIR Female %age to Total	PAJIR Female %age of Bidi Workers	PAJIR Child
I	74.3	73.3	63.3	—	83.3	81.8	54.5	—
II	73.1	91.3	78.3	2.8	91.7	100.0	100.0	13.3
III	71.4	87.5	87.5	—	75.0	100.0	66.7	—
IV	80.0	90.9	81.8	—	75.0	86.7	73.3	33.3
Sub-average	74.0	83.3	73.6	1.2	83.3	90.0	72.5	12.1
V	100.0	100.0	90.1	—	59.1	100.0	83.0	13.3
VI	75.0	85.7	85.7	14.3	50.0	75.0	58.3	50.0

VII	25.0	75.0	75.0	25.0	60.0	100.0	65.7	—
VIII	70.0	75.0	75.0	—	17.6	88.5	80.8	14.3
Sub-average	66.7	85.3	82.3	8.8	41.0	91.7	80.6	17.8
Average	72.1	84.0	76.4	3.5	58.8	91.0	77.7	15.4

Labour Utilisation

The seasonality factor might contribute to occupational differences in this district as elsewhere The monsoon months (June to September) represent peak agricultural season and so bidi-rolling may demand a lower proportion of workers during this period.

The average mandays utilised in the case of male workers in Ullal is 240.6 days, and for female workers it is 235 days. In the part-time households, male mandays utilised are comparatively higher than in the full-time households, whereas it is vice-versa in the case of female workers and also children. There is no uniform trend across the different size groups; in groups IV and VII, male labour utilisation is very low. Female labour seems to be evenly utilised in all the size groups except in I. As regards child labour, the rate of utilisation is fairly high ranging from 220 to 253 days per annum.

It is customary to take 280 days as the optimal labour utilisation rate according to many national and international standards. Though in the case of bidi-rolling, the ratio is down by over 15 per cent, increased hours of working per day seem to compensate for it. The average working hours per day in the case of male and female workers put together is over nine. If this is standardised into regular working hours, the bidi-rollers would seem to be optimally employed in different activities. Moreover, in some of the cases, there could be chances of under-reporting of labour utilisation.

In Pajir, utilisation of male labour is slightly lower than that in Ullal; so also the case with female workers. Table 4.4 highlights the mandays utilised per year across the different size groups for male, female and child labour. It is seen in both the sample areas, utilisation of male labour is higher in part-time bidi-rolling, whereas female labour is utilised to a greater extent in the full-time households. This supports the contention that in full-time households, it is predominantly the female members who constitute the bulk of bidi-rollers.

Labour Use in Ullal

Tables 4 5 and 4.6 describe the season-wise and group-wise labour utilisation in bidi-rolling and other activities in Ullal. Labour use in bidi-rolling is very low during the first season, when bulk of the labour may be in demand by agriculture. During the second season, the rate of utilisation increases tremendously and in the next season, it is still higher. The trend across the season is common to all the size groups. The full-time households have a higher rate of utilisation when compared to the part-timers. Female workers in the VI group put in over 258 days of work and the male workers over 256 days in VII group. In the latter group, female labour, along with child workers, is utilised at a higher rate (253 days for both female and child labour). During the third season, labour utilisation is highest in all the cases.

As already noted, in Ullal, besides bidi-rolling, there are other enterprises which demand seasonal as well as non-seasonal labour. However, the average labour used in other activities is lower for male workers than in bidi-rolling. Though a small proportion of female labour is utilised for other activities, their rate of utilisation seems to be quite high. Some households combine bidi-rolling with fishing, wage labour agriculture labour, or small business. In the case of activities where organisation is involved, labour utilisation in mandays is invariably low owing to stipulated working days and hours. Hence, work in organised industry may not be compared with bidi-rolling in a strict sense. Moreover, a part of the bidi-rolling time might have been expended in household chores also.

During the first season, some of the bidi-rollers may find competitive employment in other activities like agriculture. They may turn back to bidi-rolling when demand for the same would increase in other seasons.

Labour Use in Pajir

As regards male labour utilisation, the rate is higher in Pajir than in Ullal. This is so for other activities also. Female labour use is more or less similar as regards bidi-rolling but for other activities, it is lower in Pajir, Normally, most of the size groups, except the lower income ones, report even and spread-out labour use at a higher magnitude. A larger proportion of male labour utilisation in the rural sample suggests that alternative job opportunities are limited in the latter case. Agriculture is the only other occupation worth-mentioning For females, the working hours seem to be more or less similar in both the cases. The full-timers have larger working days than the part-timers

Table 4.4 : Average Mandays Per Year (all activities)

Size Group	ULLAL			PAJIR		
	Male	Female	Child	Male	Female	Child
I	258.34	212.61	220.00	243.60	205.23	—
II	233.35	245.75	220 00	223.26	230.00	200.00
III	239.60	239.72	—	250.66	201.99	—
IV	196.50	244.80	—	262.66	227.66	240.00
Sub-average	243.23	232.74	220.00	240 07	218.32	220 00
V	218 00	229 90	—	233.07	221.02	190 00
VI	247.66	258 33	220.00	255.99	259.44	256 00

VII	208.00	253.98	253.00	197.32	225.25	—
VIII	237.84	237.88	—	250 66	252.25	240.00
Sub-average	231 61	240.68	242.00	234.07	237.59	233 50
Average	240 57	235 33	236.50	237.26	230.79	229.00

Table 4.5 : Bidi Workers in Ullal

(Mandays)

Size Group	Male				Female				Child			
	S1	S2	S3	Total	S1	S2	S3	Total	S1	S2	S3	Total
I	—	—	—	—	52.20	86 78	88.36	227.34	—	—	—	—
II	57.66	90 33	95.66	243 65	52.27	91.05	95 38	238.70	40.00	90.00	90.00	220.00
III	—	—	—	—	52.28	92.57	94.71	239.56	—	—	—	—
IV	—	—	—	—	51.55	96.00	96.00	243 55	—	—	—	—
V	48.00	96 00	96.00	240.00	49.30	90.30	90.30	229.90	—	—	—	—
VI	—	—	—	—	67 33	95.50	95.50	258.33	40.00	90.00	90.00	222.00
VII	64 00	96.00	96.00	256 00	62 66	95.50	95 50	253.66	62.00	95.50	95.50	253.00
VIII	48 85	93.42	95 57	237.84	52.00	95.44	95.44	237.88	—	—	—	—

S 1=Season I—June to September.
S 2=Season II—October to January.
S 3=Season III—February to May.

Table 4.6 : Other Workers in Ullal

(Mandays)

Size Group	Male S 1	Male S 2	Male S 3	Male Total	Female S 1	Female S 2	Female S 3	Female Total
I	79.50	89.23	89.60	258 33	70.00	70.00	70.00	210.00
II	70.31	80.50	80.50	231.31	103 00	103.00	103.00	309.00
III	68.40	84.00	87.20	239.60	—	—	—	—
IV	60.50	68.00	68 00	196.50	64.00	96.00	96.00	256 00
V	45.00	58.75	58.75	162.50	—	—	—	—
VI	57.00	95.33	95.33	247.66	—	—	—	—
VII	—	80.00	80.00	160.00	—	—	—	—
VIII	—	—	—	—	—	—	—	—

S 1 = Season I—June to September.
S 2 = Season II—October to January.
S 3 = Season III—February to May.

in both the samples. The average working hours per day do not show much difference across the seasons, but the third season has slightly higher working hours. The average working hours per day in case of part-timers are 8.88 in Ullal and 8.52 in Pajir; for full-timers the average increases to 9.58 in the former, and 9.06 in the latter. It is seen that female labour has to put extra hours of work in the rural sample. Perhaps the implication of this may be better explained in relation to productivity to be discussed shortly.

Table 4.7 and 4.8 present the utilisation of mandays in bidi and other activities sex-wise, group-wise and season-wise. To a certain extent, what was noticed in Ullal is also present in Pajir-lower labour demand for bidi-rolling during first season. In some cases, the average mandays reported are lower in Pajir than in Ullal for female workers. A peculiar aspect in Pajir is the higher rate of utilisation of child labour.

Labour Productivity

The analysis pertaining to labour productivity in bidi-rolling largely considers female labour, since it shares the major burden of work. It was already noted that over three fourths of bidi-rollers in both Ullal and Pajir are female workers. Moreover, male and child workers report activity only in some size groups. Hence female labour has been considered to evaluate bidi productivity.

Table 4.9 describes the season-wise labour productivity in Ullal and Pajir according to different income groups. On the whole, it is seen that labour productivity expressed in terms of bidis rolled per day, is slightly lower in the first season, irrespective of the regions. It should be noted that the low productivity is noticed mainly in the case of part-time households. It could be that, having recourse to greater opportunities in the monsoon season, the part-timers might give a lower rate of preference to bidi-rolling. This would be amply highlighted when comparing the income productivities between the categories.

The feature of low productivity is not peculiar only to the first season. In Ullal, in other seasons also the performance of part-timers is 5 to 8 per cent lower than the season average for all bidi-rollers. In Pajir, average for the part-timers is very low; perhaps the peak agricultural season might have a say in this.

The rate of efficiency increases from first to second and from second to third season in both semi-urban and rural areas. The full-timers manage to perform about 15 per cent more efficiently than the part-timers in Ullal. In Pajir, the proportion is around 10 per cent, suggesting that the semi-urban sample attaches a greater importance to productivity. Nonetheless, the wage rate existing there is higher by about 8 to 10 per cent than in Pajir. Also, competition between different callings compel a better productive structure in employment to be evolved.

The average quantity of bidis rolled per day in Ullal is about 643, whereas, it is 668 in Pajir. For the part-timers, the productivity is 603 and 621 bidis per day respectively in the samples. For the full-timers, the average productivity is higher in Ullal (714) than in Pajir (692), suggesting, as noted earlier, a greater awareness in the Ullal sample on alternate productive structures. During the first season, the productivity of part-timers in Pajir is lower than that in Ullal; for other seasons, Pajir part-timers report a higher productivity. The full-timers report a lower productivity in Pajir during the first as well as the second seasons. It is only during the third season that they are able to register some increase in productivity. During that season, the main occupation in the area is bidi-rolling only.

Since working hours vary in both the regions and also across the income groups, female labour productivity has been computed on hour basis also, i.e. bidis rolled per hour, showing differences as presented in Table 4.10. It is found that the average working hours per day in Ullal is 9.13, whereas it is 8.91 in Pajir. The corresponding quantity of bidis rolled per hour is 70.4 in Ullal and 75.0 in Pajir. Working hours and productivity are both higher in full-time bidi-rolling households in both the areas. The average productivity for the full-time households is 74.5 bidis in Ullal and 76.4 bidis in Pajir. The difference between the regions is low for part-timers, 7 per cent greater in Pajir. Income groups III, V, and VII in Ullal and III, VI and VII in Pajir roll more than 80 bidis per hour. The first group in both the areas produce the lowest quantity on bidis. The VI followed by group IV in Ullal also falls into this categorry. When we compare total households in these different income groups, group I in Ullal, owing to a large number of households in it performs less efficiently than the rest. It would be noted

Table 4.7 : Bidi Workers in Pajir

(*Mandays*)

Size Group	Male				Female				Child			
	S 1	*S 2*	*S 3*	*Total*	*S 1*	*S 2*	*S 3*	*Total*	*S 1*	*S 2*	*S 3*	*Total*
I	—	—	—	—	61.33	72.00	72.00	205.33	—	—	—	—
II	—	—	—	—	54.00	80.00	96.00	230.00	48.00	72.00	80.00	200.00
III	—	—	—	—	60.00	82 50	96.00	238.50	—	—	—	—
IV	96.00	96 00	96.00	288.00	66.90	86.90	93 09	246 89	48 00	96.00	96.00	240 00
V	81.00	88.00	96.00	265.00	56 66	79.33	88 66	224 65	39.00	63.00	88.00	190.00
VI	80.00	80.00	80.00	240.00	57.14	91.42	96 00	244.56	64 00	96.00	96.00	256.00
VII	—	—	—	—	53.33	80 00	96.00	229 33	—	—	—	—
VIII	58.66	96.00	96.00	250.66	52.38	91.14	94.85	238.37	48.00	96.00	96.00	240.00

S 1 = Season I—June to September.
S 2 = Season II—October to January.
S 3 = Season III—February to May.

Table 4.8 : Other Workers in Pajir

(*Mandays*)

Size Group	*Male*				*Female*			
	S1	*S2*	*S3*	*Total*	*S1*	*S2*	*S3*	*Total*
I	81.20	81.20	81.20	243 60	72.00	72.00	61.33	205.33
II	68.36	86.90	68.11	223.37	—	—	—	—
III	80.00	85.33	85.33	250.66	68.00	60.00	12.00	140.00
IV	89.60	89.60	76.60	256.80	34.00	42.00	40.00	116.00
V	76.44	85.09	88.40	249.93	80.00	80.00	95.00	256.00
VI	88.00	88.00	88.00	264.00	87.00	87.00	48.00	222.00
VII	74.66	74.66	48.00	197.32	60.00	70.00	70.00	200.00
VIII	—	—	—	—	93.00	93.00	93.00	279.00

S 1 = Season I — June to September.
S 2 = Season II — October to January.
S 3 = Season III — February to May.

Table 4.9 : Season-wise Female Labour Productivity (bidis per day)

Size Group	*Season 1*		*Season 2*		*Season 3*		*Average*	
	U	*P*	*U*	*P*	*U*	*P*	*U*	*P*
I	462.2	482.6	511.4	548.1	528.0	548.1	506.5	528.6
II	621.6	655.6	664.1	662.5	657.5	745.3	652.1	695.4
III	769.5	580.0	753.1	717.6	736.1	725.0	750.0	711.3
IV	612.1	513.1	592.6	575.8	592.6	640.6	596.7	583.3
Sub average	582.4	555.3	609.0	613.5	610.4	662.0	603.4	620.3
V	754.1	650.1	774.7	654.8	754.8	728.3	762.5	682.7
VI	612.6	800.0	811.5	750.0	588.2	814.3	678.0	787.0

VII	861.8	800.0	726.0	753.3	726.0	711.1	760.0	746.5
VIII	637.6	621.1	652.6	655.4	639.2	676.4	664.0	656.2
Sub-average	698.3	673.2	740.6	676.6	695.2	718.1	713.6	692.3
Average	623.8	633.9	656.0	644.6	640.7	699.4	642.8	663.4

U = Ullal ; P = Pajir.

Table 4.10 : Female Labour Productivity in Bidi-rolling

Size Group	*ULLAL*		*PAJIR*	
	Hrs/day	*Bidis/hr*	*Hrs/day*	*Bidis/hr*
I	8.33	60.80	8 41	62 85
II	9.16	71.19	9.27	75 02
III	9.20	81.52	8.83	80 55
IV	9.25	64.51	7.93	73.56
Sub-average	8.88	67.95	8.52	72.83
V	9.20	82.88	8.99	75.94
VI	11.25	60.27	9 08	86.67
VII	9.00	84.44	9 17	81.40
VIII	9.04	73.45	9.11	72.03
Sub-average	9.58	74.49	9.06	76 41
Average	9 13	70.40	8.91	75.02

that in this group, 19 per cent of the total income is accounted by bidi-rolling. In Pajir on the other hand, the income groups having large samples in them report average and more than average productivity.

Notwithstanding the above, the average productivity is higher in the rural sample as is highlighted by Tables 4.9 and 4.10. The part-timers in a rural sector seem to perform efficiently than their semi-urban counterparts. The full-timers there performing slightly less efficiently might indicate that there could be some opening for them to be distracted from their activities in search of employment in urban areas. This, coupled with other locational factors might have resulted in low productivity.

The season-wise bidi productivity for male labour is slightly higher than that of female labour in both the regions. It is found that a male worker rolls about 10 per cent more bidis per hour than a female in Ullal. The seasonwise average productivity comes to 74.5, 82.1, and 83.2 bidis per hour in the three seasons. Here also, the full-timers have a higher productivity than the part-timers. In Pajir also, male labour productivity is quite responsive to full-time as well as part-time bidi-rolling. On average, it is about 6 to 7 per cent higher than that of female bidi productivity. Excepting the second season, (78 bidis per hour) male labour in Pajir has a higher performance ratio (79.0 and 33.5 bidis in the first and third seasons) than female labour and also its counterpart in Ullal.

The wage rate for bidi-rolling in Ullal has been about Rs 13.43 per 1000 bidis, inclusive of all benefits (amounting to about 20 per cent of basic wages) during the recent times. The basic wage rate of 10.88 per 1000 bidis has been existing since last year. The proportion of benefits vary from 20 to 25 per cent according to the manipulations of the contractors. Unregistered rollers may not get any benefits beyond the basic wages; similar is the case with child labour below 15 years of age. In certain cases, child production may be shown against registered members in the family for convenience of calculating of benefits.

Also, the wage rates differ from place to place. The minimum wage rate if it is fixed at Rs 8.90, would vary from that level (in interior rural areas) to Rs 10.88 (in urban areas). For example, the average wage rate existing in Pajir during the reference period was Rs 10.10 per 1000 bidis rolled and other admissible benefits, whereas it has been higher at Ullal. In Pajir, the workers will get a wage rate of Rs 12.44 per 1000 bidis rolled inclusive of all benefits, as against Rs 13.43 in Ullal.

As already noted, an average female in Ullal produces 643 bidis per day and would get Rs 8.50 as wages. If the same worker opts for agriculture or other work she would get a minimum of Rs 9.00 per day. Hence, the opportunity cost for women seem to be very limited. This is the case with the Pajir women also. Male workers, on the other hand, could get a daily wage rate of over Rs 15.00 for agriculture or more for other activities, whereas they could produce bidis worth about Rs 9.00 to

Table 4.11 : Household and Per Worker Bidi and Total Income (Ullal)

(*Rs/P.A.*)

Size Group	*Household Bidi Income*	*Household Other Income*	*Household Total Income*	*Per Worker Bidi Income*	*Per Worker Total Income*	*Per Capita Income*
I	2,099	9,70	11,169	1,547	3,258	1,737
II	4,155	8,303	12,458	2,126	3,384	1,612
III	3,378	3,920	7,298	2,413	3,041	1,303
IV	4,392	4,100	8,492	1,952	2,426	1,068
Sub-average	3,222	7,480	10,702	1,939	3,178	1,617
V	5,200	3,467	8,667	2,364	2,708	1,806
VI	5,372	2,228	7,600	2,479	2,400	1,267

VII	6,567	1,500	8,067	2,627	3,227	949
VIII	5,749	—	5,749	2,875	2,875	1,394
Sub-average	5,625	1,501	7,126	2,630	2,759	1,394
Average	4,053	5,411	9,464	2,218	3,063	1,552

Table 4.12 : Household and Per Worker Bidi and Total Income (Pajir)

(*Rs/P A*)

Size Group	*Household Bidi Income*	*Household Other Income*	*Household Total Income*	*Per Worker Bidi Income*	*Per Worker Total Income*	*Per Capita Income*
I	2,025	5,766	7,791	1,350	2,226	1,154
II	2,719	5,418	8,137	1,813	2,441	1,395
III	4,070	5,742	9,812	2,035	2,180	1,635
IV	4,837	4,057	8,894	1,860	2,224	1,533
Sub-average	3,336	5,139	8,475	1,772	2,287	1,399
V	4,685	2,935	7,6[illegible]0	1,909	2,044	1,310
VI	6,130	2,240	8,370	2,581	2,480	1,395

VII	6,389	1,200	7,589	2,130	1,518	1,012
VIII	5,101	2.158	5,259	2,000	1,912	822
Sub-average	5,179	2,387	6,854	2,056	2,012	1,108
Average	4,467	3,13	7,480	1,966	2,044	1,219

Table 4.13 : Semi-urban and Rural Workers

Particulars		Semi-urban				Rural			
		Part-time	*Lowest*	*Full-time*	*Highest*	*Part-time*	*Lowest*	*Full-time*	*Highest*
Family size		6.6	6.4	5.1	4.1	6.1	6.7	6.2	6.4
Bidi workers :	Female %	92.9	100.0	70.0	56.3	85.3	100.0	80.6	77.8
	Child %	1.8	—	7.5	—	11.8	—	11.1	11.1
	Male %	5.3	—	22.5	—	2.9	—	8.3	11.1
Mandayr/year :	Female	236.0	227.3	244.7	237.9	230.2	205.3	234.2	238.4
	Child	220.0	—	236.5	—	220.0	—	228.7	240.0
	Male	243.6	—	244.6	—	228.0	—	251.9	250.7

Hours worked/day :	Female	8.88	8.33	9.58	9.04	8.52	8.41	9.06	9.11
	Child	8.00	—	6.50	—	7.50	—	7.66	8 60
	Male	9.00	—	9.10	9.20	10.00	—	9.81	10.00

Note : Part-time bidi households indicate contribution of bidi income less than 60%; full-time households indicate more than that; 'Lowest' indicate less than 30% contribution by bidi income and 'Highest' over 90%.

Rs 9.70 only. This is also a reason for low proportion of male workers reported in bidi-rolling. It has been noticed that handicapped or sickly male workers prefer to remain attached to bidi-rolling. In many cases, the males were either disabled or disinterested in other activities. In some cases, men and children were assisting the female workers.

Income Structure

Household bidi income has been calculated taking into consideration the total bidi production as reported according to different seasons. Income from other activities (other income) has been calculated considering the income reported from activities other than bidi-rolling. Total income consists of bidi income and other income. Per worker bidi and total income and per capita total income have also been calculated for the areas (Tables 4.11 and 4.12).

In Ullal, the average household bidi income is Rs 4053, whereas it is Rs 4467 in Pajir. As was the case with productivity, the average bidi income is higher in the full-time units Rs 5625 vs Rs 3222 and Rs 5179 vs Rs 3336 respectively. The average other income shows a larger magnitude in the part-time bidi households (Rs 7480 and Rs 5139) in Ullal and Pajir respectively.

In Ullal, the first group reports about 19 per cent of the total income as obtainable from bidi-rolling. The proportion increases 33 per cent 42 per cent and 52 per cent for the succeeding income groups. For the part-time units as a whole, bidi income accounts for about 30 per cent of the total. For the Pajir sample, this sub-average is about 40 per cent. For the full-timers, the average share of bidi income is about 79 per cent in Ullal and 76 per cent in Pajir. For the entire sample 43.0 per cent of the total income in Ullal has been from bidi-rolling. The percentage increases to about 60 in Pajir. In the latter sample, bidi income has a higher share although per household total income is higher in Ullal, owing to larger share by other activities.

The per worker bidi income has been Rs 2218 in Ullal and Rs 1966 in Pajir, though total workers are more or less same in both the regions (95 and 100 respectively). The number of part-time units are more in Ullal and in Pajir it is the full-timers. Hence, average per worker income is higher in Ullal. The per worker bidi income in the full-time bidi households is quite high, more so in Ullal. Owing to better opportunity cost for other activities in Ullal, the per worker total income is substantially higher. In this case, it is in the part-time units that such a substantial increase is noticed. In Pajir also, other income has an edge over bidi income, especially in part-time units. Even after allowing for a margin of 10 to 15 per cent as difference in the wage rates, Ullal would still dominate in income contribution from other activities.

Per capita income (non-standardised) has been calculated taking into consideration total members in the family. The per capita income is Rs 1552 in Ullal and Rs 1219 in Pajir. Groups I, II, and V report above than the average income in Ullal and groups III and IV in Pajir. Group VII in Ullal and group VIII in Pajir seem to perform below average. More of this will be explained in comparison to standardised per capita expenditure in the next chapter, wherein a ratio of 1.2 is to be taken as the multiplier, to make the above per capita income standardised.

An attempt is made to group the samples into 'lowest' (less than 30 per cent bidi contribution) and 'highest' (over 90 per cent bidi contribution). in addition to part-time and full-time households. Table 4.13 presents the family size, composition of bidi workers, mandays and hours worked per day. Family size is lowest in the 'highest' group and also female workers, but not child and male workers. There are no significant differences in mandays worked but in hours worked per day, especially in the case of male workers, they are higher in the 'highest' group. For females, except in rural 'highest', the hours are lower in the other groups. A significant finding is that children also work for 6.5 to 8.6 hours with full capacity wherever they are opportunity earners.

Table 4.14 describes bidi productivity (no. of bidis, rolled per day and hour) wherein the 'lowest' and 'highest' groups perform less efficiently in the case of female labour. Male labour is efficient only in the semi-urban 'highest' group. Child labour performs less efficiently in rural 'highest' group. Bidi wastage is higher in 'lowest' and lower in 'highest' semi-urban groups. In the rural areas, it is the opposite of this. Declining bidi

Table 4.14 : Bidi Productivity in Semi-urban and Rural Samples

Productivity	Semi-urban				Rural			
	Port-time	*Lowest*	*Full-time*	*Higheet*	*Part-time*	*Lowest*	*Full-time*	*Highest*
Bidis/day: Female:	603.4	506.5	713.6	664.0	620.5	528.6	692.6	656.0
Child :	454.5	—	372.7	—	248.4	—	415.0	400.0
Male :	680.8	—	798.8	847.6	833.3	—	735.1	610.7
Bidis/hour: Female:	68.0	60.8	74.5	73.5	72.8	62.9	76.4	72.1
Child :	56.8	—	57.3	—	33.1	—	54.2	46.5
Male :	75.6	--	87.7	92.1	83.3	—	74.9	61.1
Bidi wastage % :	5.12	5.31	4.53	4.08	4.92	5.01	4.24	4.96

productivity may be related to higher percentage of wastage which is 5.01 in 'lowest' and 4.96 per cent in 'highest' bidi households in the rural areas. In the semi-urban area also, lower bidi productivity in the 'lowest' group may be related to higher percentage of wastage (5.31 per cent).

5

CONSUMPTION EXPENDITURE

Introduction

The difference between the highest and the lowest per capita income levels has been about 50 to 60 per cent in bidi as well as total income. Excepting the first group in both the samples, the variation in per capita bidi income is not much. Five of the eight income groups in Ullal and six in Pajir seem to be closer to the average. As regards per worker total income, most of the income groups report low variation. Because of this feature, it would be very difficult to encounter different consumption standards either. Of course, the income level as determining the consumption standard, is different for the full-time as well as part-time bidi households. This should give some interesting results on consumption and lifestyle patterns between the groups.

Particulars have been collected on total household expenditure covering food, health, education, fuel and other types of expenditure during the reference year. In food consumption, an attempt has been made to evaluate daily per capita protein and calorie consumption.

In calculating the per capita expenditure, the total members of the households have been standardised. The standardised units across the different groups are shown in Tables 4.1 and 4.2. After standardisation, (male adult) consumption units form about 82 per cent of the family members in Ullal and 84 per cent in Pajir. For this, one female unit has been taken equal to 0.9 male unit and 1 child unit to 0.6 male unit. Hence, when we compare this with the per capita income, we should multiply that by a factor of 1.2 in both the samples to get the income standardised. When this is accomplished, the proportion of per capita income spent on consumption would be about 67 per cent in Ullal and 88 per cent in Pajir.

Since it was not possible to get consumption patterns according to different individual family members, the total family expenditure has been standardised into standard male units.

Table 5.1 presents the total expenditure pattern for Ullal sample. For the entire sample, expenditure on food forms about 57 per cent of total expenditure. Expenditure on health is about

Table 5.1 : Per Capita Food, Health, Education and Total Expenditure

(ULLAL)
(Rs/Year)

Size Group	*Food Exp.*	*Health Exp.*	*Education Exp.*	*Fuel Exp.*	*Other Exp.*	*Total Exp.*
I	1,054.9	100 8	27.9	138 6	589 9	1,912.1
II	930.8	69 8	12.5	142.5	482.6	1,638.2
III	992.8	27.5	53 4	173 8	392.4	1,639 9
IV	1,067.5	51.9	16.2	124 4	547.9	1,808 0
Sub-average	1,002.6	75.8	24.1	141 9	523.5	1,767.9
V	1,047 7	141.1	7.6	220 9	651 3	2,068.8
VI	883 3	143.4	7.0	153.3	258 3	1,445.2
VII	843 2	40.3	7.5	100 0	324 9	1,315.9
VIII	824 9	52.6	3.7	205.7	332.2	1,419.1
Sub-average	898.0	91.3	6.1	180.8	400.3	1,576.4
Average	972.5	80.2	18.9	153.0	488.2	1,712 9

5 per cent, on education a mere one per cent and on fuel about 9 per cent. The rest is accounted for by other items of expenditure—clothes, recreation, transport and communication and other household purchases. Among the part-timers also, food expenditure accounts for about 57 per cent of the total expenditure. Only group V seems to expend about 50 per cent of total expenditure on food. In this group, the average health expenditure is about 6.8 per cent. The only other group which exceeds in health expenditure is the sixth, where the proportion increases to about 10 per cent. In education, all the households report a low expenditure level. The households seem to expend on other items without significant differences among them

In contrast to semi-urban sample, in Pajir, food accounts for about 73 per cent of total expenditure (Table 5.2). Here food and health (the latter sharing about 7 per cent of total expenditure) are the major expenditure items. Education and fuel account for less than 1.4 and 3 per cent respectively. The share of other expenditure is only 16 per cent whereas it is over 28 per cent in Ullal. In Ullal, total per capita expenditure is about 56 per cent of per capita total income, whereas, it is 74 per cent in Pajir. When the consumption units are not standardised, the proportions would increase to 67 and 88 per cent respectively in the areas,

There is little difference between the full-time and part-time households in allocating total expenditure on food. The full-timers spend slightly higher on health and also on education but less on fuel when compared to the part-timers. The size groups show very low levels of expenditure in education. There could be a possibility that child labour (below 15 years of age) is utilised in household and other activities but not reported otherwise. Generally, the bidi households are poor and as income grows, women-folk tend to attach less importance to bidi-rolling. So, in poor households where bidi-rolling is a supplementary form of earning, no wonder children are looked upon as money-spinners.

The Standard of Living

We may consider the standard of living of the full-time and part-time households. Though not much difference could be noticed between some groups, it has been possible to bring out

Table 5.2 : Per Capita Food, Health, Education and Total Expenditure

(PAJIR)
(Rs/Year)

Size Group	*Food Exp.*	*Health Exp.*	*Education Exp.*	*Fuel Exp.*	*Other Exp.*	*Total Exp.*
I	834.2	63 0	20.6	67.4	240.5	1,234.7
II	1,058.5	110.6	12.4	43.8	205.9	1,431.2
III	821.3	84.9	14.2	20.6	270.4	1,211.4
IV	1,354.2	102.8	12 0	45.1	292.5	1,806.6
Sub-total	1,062 2	93.0	14.6	47.3	246.6	1,463.7
V	1,084.1	106.3	23.5	48.5	178.5	1,440.9
VI	1,270.2	102.9	6.1	51.7	266.5	1,697.4
VII	974.6	59.5	19.0	29.7	304.2	1,387.0
VIII	1,131.5	131.3	34 4	38.1	279.7	1,615.0
Sub-total	1,116.9	110.8	24.6	43.4	242.2	1,537.2
Total	1,095.0	104.1	20.3	44.9	245.2	1,510.0

the differences in food and fuel consumption and also on the savings behaviour among them.

First, we begin with the asset structure. In the semi-urban area, about 40 per cent of the households own houses, whereas in the rural sample over 75 per cent units own houses. The migratory nature of rural labour into urban areas might be a reason for low proportion of owned houses there. About 40 per cent of the houses in Ullal and 14 per cent in Pajir have been electrified. The assets include items such as furniture, radio and transistor, watches and clocks, etc. The immovable property has not been considered in the asset structure. The per capita asset holding is Rs 620 in Ullal and Rs 310 in Pajir. The part-timers in Ullal have a higher asset holding than the full-timers. In Pajir, both the classes have more or less similar asset position.

About 38 per cent of the households have wells in their own premises in Ullal and the percentage is 34 in Pajir. About 36 per cent of the sample population in Ullal are literates. Only about 1.5 per cent of the people have studied up to high school and above level. About 27 per cent of the families in Ullal regularly read newspapers and listen to radio. In Pajir, people reading newspapers is lower than those who listen to radio (43 per cent).

About 56 per cent of the households in Ullal and 77 per cent in Pajir belong to bidi labour unions. Normally, the unions are affiliated to C.I.T.U in both regions. Very few of the members participate actively in union activities. The unionisation of bidi labour in this part of the state is very strong, as in Kerala. Because of this, the wage rates have increased in recent years. Over the past 6 to 7 years, money wage rate has more than doubled.

A major disadvantage in bidi-rolling is the occurrence of tobacco-induced diseases among the rollers. It has been noticed that continuous bidi-rolling has disabled some workers' eyesight and also resulted in some cases of T.B. and other severe health complications. Only about 40 per cent of the households report normal health in Ullal. About 10 per cent of the households report chronic health problems. In Pajir, though not many chronic cases were observed, most of the workers complained one or other diseases. Some of the bidi manufacturers have established health clinics to look after the bidi workers but very few people seem to go to such clinics. They usually prefer quick-healing private clinic treatment. In the semi-urban area, it is mostly government hospitals where the workers go for free medical treatment. In some cases, they go to private (including ayurvedic) doctors. As has been highlighted. per capita health expenditure is higher in Pajir and especially in the full time bidi households (Table 4.2). This would mean that full-time bidi-rollers are exposed to grave health problems due to inhaling of tobacco flakes and bidi leaves. Also, sitting constantly for longer hours to roll bidi might result in other body disorders.

Here we have to consider some cases where some male bidi-rollers smoke a portion of bidis they roll even without proper healing. In some cases, consumption of 50 or more bidis per day has been reported. It is common to find workers and also management of a bidi company adhering to the particular brand of bidi for smoking.

In Ullal, according to a study undertaken by the Karnataka Urban Water Supply and Drainage Board during 1979-80, it was found that about 90 per cent of the people surveyed had T.B. and also filariasis. The intensity of the disease was equally distributed among males and females and the effect ranged from +1 to +60, the latter signifying a very high intensity. According to the Indian Council for Medical Research, one in three Indians faces the risk of filariasis, a disease which may not be fatal but disables the person permanently. In India, about 15 million people suffer from this disease. More people can get the infection without showing the symptoms. This disease is concentrated largely to coastal areas. It may happen that people, disabled because of this disease, would turn to bidi-rolling in coastal areas like Ullal.

Food Consumption

Expenditure on food consumption has been analysed into per capita protein and calorie consumption, and daily expenditure on food (Table 5.3). An attempt has been made here to evaluate the energy obtained by food consumption. The norm of 2,400 k.cal as the daily minimum nutritional standard in rural areas has been reported in the rural sample. On the other hand, in the semi-urban sample, the daily per capita calorie consumption seems to be low at around 2043 k.cal. The per capita protein consumption is also high in the rural sample at 62 gms per day as against 56.5 gms in the semi-urban sample. It seems that the effective efficiency of food uptake is higher in the rural area. This is also evidenced by the fact that per every rupee spent on food consumption, the rural households seem to derive a better alimentation, though in case of protein the increase is just in correspondence with the increase in the unit expenditure.

Table 5.3 : Per Capita Protein and Calorie Consumption

Size Group	*ULLAL*			*PAJIR*		
	*1**	*2@*	*3&*	*1**	*2@*	*3&*
I	2.89	62.0	2,226.0	2.31	45.4	1,746.7
II	2.55	53.8	1,917.2	2.90	59.1	2,412.6
III	2.72	56.0	2,158.6	2.25	49.3	1,948.5
IV	2.92	62.2	2,336.6	3.71	76.3	3,101.2
Sub-total	2.75	58.2	2,112.2	2.91	59.4	2,386.7
V	2.90	61.4	2,204.6	2.97	62.6	2,352.8
VI	2.42	55 2	2,031.0	3.48	73.6	2,922.8
VII	2.31	44.1	1,745.4	2.67	58.0	2,288.4
VIII	2.26	48.7	1 612.8	3.10	62.0	2,573.2
Sub-total	2.46	52.3	1,867.0	3.06	63.5	2,582.3
Total	2.67	56.5	2,043.4	3.00	62.0	2,509.2

* Per capita food expenditure (Rs/day)
@ Per capita protein consumption (gms/day)
& Per capita calorie consumption (K.cal/day)

In Ullal, the part-timers spend more on food—by about 12 per cent higher than the full-timers. For that, they get about 11 per cent more protein and 13 per cent more calories than the full-timers. This would mean that they are slightly efficient in calorie consumption. Possibly, food consumed by the full-timers does not contain adequate nutrients. It could be also that full-time bidi-rolling may not demand as much energy as would be for other activities. Size groups VII and VIII (where households depend for more than 80 per cent of their income by bidi-rolling) report very low protein and calorie consumption. Groups I, IV and V have a better nutritional standard than others.

In Pajir, on the other hand, it is the full-timers that report a higher energy consumption. The efficiency seems to be low in size groups I and V. In the rest, it seems to be uniform. In protein as well as calorie consumption, group IV followed by group VI, enjoys a better nutritional standard.

Fuel Consumption

Fuel consumption is one of the major indicators of life style. The dwindling forest resources and increasing pressure on fuel-wood has brought in an energy crisis, where it has been very difficult to augment adequate fuelwood resources. According to the National Sample Survey (18th and 28th rounds covering over a decade—1963-64 and 1973-74), the average per capita energy consumption has not changed significantly during this decade in India. Firewood constitutes over 69 per cent of all energy resources consumed in rural area, while the percentage share is 45 in urban areas. According to the report of the Working Group on Energy Policy, firewood to the extent of 12.7 per cent in rural and 73.7 per cent in urban areas is purchased and the rest is either collected or home-grown. Firewood is the chief non-commercial source of energy, the contribution of which is still substantial, though commercial energy sources are slowly making their way into the rural areas.

In the sample areas, particulars have been obtained regarding firewood consumption (both collected and home-grown and purchased); and also consumption of kerosene and electricity. Firewood includes logs, twigs, and branches, leaves, coconut fronds and shells and wastes from saw mills, etc. In a very few cases, use of animal dung as fuel was noticed in both the areas. Firewood is the major energy source for cooking food, boiling water for bathing and washing; kerosene oil is being used mainly to light oil lamps and electricity for lighting.

As has been already noted, fuel expenses constitute about 9 per cent of total expenditure in Ullal and 3 per cent in Pajir. This includes only the purchased part. The collected and home-grown part of firewood has been quite substantial in both the places. In Ullal, about half of the total firewood consumed has been bought. In Pajir, the proportion of purchased firewood is also lower. While on an average about Rs. 0.52 has been paid per kg of firewood of all types in Ullal, the price paid in Pajir has been just Rs 0.16 In the semi-urban sample, the consumers have to depend on shops for purchase of firewood In Pajir, on the other hand, though some firewood depots are existing, the bulk of the purchased part of firewood is transacted informally during rainy season when there is wear and tear in woodlots. In recent times, the price of fuelwood has increased to over Rs 0.60 to Rs 0.70 per kg Good quality fuelwood commands a very high price and is about more than one fourth of the price of rice, the common staple in the region.

The per capita consumption of firewood has been 403.? kgs in Ullal per year and ?84 9 kgs in Pajir. In Ullal, the full-timers consumed a larger quantity of firewood than the part-timers. The full-timers seem to consume more or less the same quantity of kerosene as the part-timers. On an average, about 15.7 litre of kerosene oil has been consumed by one standardised adult unit. Every household will get a fixed quantity of kerosene oil per month from the ration shop and in cases where the demand is more, it has to be bought from the private dealers at a higher price. The price per litre has been averaged at Rs 2 62 In some cases besides lighting, kerosene is used for cooking purposes also. In a few instances (Ullal), kerosene has completely replaced firewood as a cooking medium. In Ullal, about 40 per cent of the households have been electrified. The per capita electricity consumption (only for lighting purposes) has been Rs 8 2 in Ullal. Here also, not much difference could be noticed between the full-timers and part-timers (Tables 5 4 and 5 5).

In Pajir, the part-timers consume a slightly higher quantity of firewood than the full-timers. The difference in kerosene consumption is not much In Pajir, kerosene consumption is about 30 per cent lower than that in Ullal, it is used only for lighting purposes. Only group II in the part-time households consumed some electricity. But a considerable number of full-timers use it. The proportion of electrified houses in Pajir is only 14 per cent. The average electricity consumption is just Rs 3.4 (about two-fifths of Ullal level). It seems from the data, the Pajir sample consumes low energy resources—firewood, kerosene, and electricity. In Pajir, collection of twigs and

Table 5.4 : Per Capita Consumption of Fuel in Ullal Per Year

Size Group	Firewood Callected Kg	Firewood Purchased Kg	Firewood Purchased Rs P	Kerosene Li	Kerosene Rs P	Electricity Rs P	Total fuel Rs P
I	183 8	178 3	88 4	15.1	38 4	9.8	138.6
II	157.4	166.9	90.8	15.7	43.0	8.7	142.6
III	182.3	232.7	122.4	17.9	45.7	5.7	173.8
IV	194.1	156.9	81.4	13,6	37.1	5.9	124.5
Sub-total	174.9	178.4	92.6	15.5	40.5	8.5	142.0
V	329.9	329.9	165 5	15.3	39 6	15.8	220 9
VI	215.2	179 3	87 8	23.7	59 3	6.2	153.3
VII	231.4	161 6	77.6	5 2	14 3	8 1	100.0
VIII	281.2	293 9	155 0	17.5	48 5	2.2	205.7
Sub-total	269 1	257 6	130 9	16.0	42.2	7.6	180.7
Total	202.0	201.2	103.7	15.7	41.2	8 2	153.1

branches especially by children was not fully reported from the sample though it was observed during the field study. Therefore, we may add up a certain proportion to the reported firewood consumption there. Still Pajir would be consuming firewood and other resources at lower level when compared to Ullal

These figures may be compared with the 32nd round of N.S.S. conducted in Karnataka during 1977-78. The per capita monthly firewood consumption was 21.0 kgs and that of kerosene 0.5 litres. The bulk of the energy consumption has been in fuelwood only. The expenditure in the lower income

Table 5.5 : Per Capita Consumption of Fuel in Pajir Per Year

Size Group	*Firewood*			*Kerosene*		*Electricity*	*Total fuel*
	Callected	*Purchased*					
	Kg	*Kg*	*Rs P*	*Li*	*Rs P*	*Rs P*	*Rs P*
I	228.3	53.4	27.4	13.7	40.0	—	67.4
II	203.5	128.7	99.9	10.2	29.6	4 3	43.8
III	220.8	22.6	4.7	5.7	15.9	—	20.6
IV	186.5	109.2	13.2	11.8	31.9	—	45.1
Sub-total	207.0	90.7	14.7	11.0	31.2	1.4	47.3
V	162.5	99.6	18 1	8.9	23.2	7.2	48.5
VI	104.6	154.4	12 4	12 4	30.6	—	51.7
VII	199.2	39.7	1.9	8.2	22.0	5.8	29.7
VIII	267.0	42.5	5.3	11.6	29.4	3.4	38.1
Sub-total	196.6	80.6	12.3	10.3	26.5	4.6	43 4
Total	200.5	84.4	13.2	10.6	28.3	3.4	44.9

classes has been relatively low. Thus the sample findings come closer to the N.S.S findings—low per capita fuel consumption in the lower income groups and rural areas.

From that Survey, it is noticed that for all expenditure classes, the average monthly per capita expenditure was Rs 49.82, ranging from Rs 19.36 in the lowest to Rs 168.34 in the highest group. Though the picture would be different after 7 years, it could be said that little difference might be encountered in fuel and kerosene consumption now. Actually, over years the per capita fuel consumption, owing to problems

Table 5.6 : Semi-Urban and Rural Income-Expenditure Patterns

(*Rs/P A*)

Particulars	*Semi-Urban*				*Rural*			
	Part-time	*Lowest*	*Full-time*	*Highest*	*Part-time*	*Lowest*	*Full-time*	*Highest*
Per worker total income	3,178	3,258	2,759	2,875	2,228	2,226	2,012	1,912
,, bidi income	1,939	1,547	2,630	2,875	1,772	1,350	2,056	2,000
Per capita total income	1,617	1,737	1,394	1,3 4	1,399	1,154	1,108	822
Per capita expenditure	1,473	1,593	1,313	1,183	1,220	1,029	1,282	1,345
— ,, % spent on : food	56 7	55.2	57.0	58.1	72.6	67.6	72.6	70.1
,, : health	4.3	5.3	5.8	3.7	6.3	5.1	7.2	8.1
,, : education	1.4	1 5	0.4	0.3	1.0	1.7	1.2	2.1
,, : fuel	8.0	7.3	11.5	14.5	3.2	5.5	2 8	2.4
Calorie consumption : K.cal/p.c/day	2,112	2,226	1,867	1,613	2,387	1,747	2,582	2,353
Savings rate (%)	8.9	8.3	5.8	15.1	12.8	10.8	—15.7	—63.6
Per capita borrowings	216	336	233	248	245	110	331	214

in collection, effective demand, etc. may decline also. But in our survey, the per capita fuel consumption is slightly higher than the figures given above. The per capita fuelwood consumption ranged from 142.2 kgs to 5'1.2 kgs in our survey. It has ranged from 238.9 kgs to 3 2.2 kgs in Pajir, a rural sample, showing a lower degree of variation.

Table 5.6 presents income and expenditure patterns for the 'lowest', part-time, full-time and 'highest' groups of households. When bidi share is the 'lowest', it performs slightly better in the case of semi-urban total income, but not in bidi income and in rural area, it performs poorer in both the situations. Per capita expenditure is, however, higher in the 'lowest' than the part-time and not much difference noted in consumption expenditure save in food where it is more efficient. The savings rate is lower in the 'lowest' cases. This is more or less the case with regard to rural 'highest' when compared to full-time bidi households there. This suggests that too lower or higher the bidi share in household income, the economics is not favourable, which suggests that a via media wherein many activities are undertaken should bring in an optimal income—expenditure ratio. Savings rate in the rural full-time and especially in the 'highest' groups is significantly negative and viewed from the low capacity to borrow, the problem of those groups assumes crucial significance. In the semi-urban 'highest', the savings rate is quite substantial and income-expenditure rate favourable. An interesting point to note is that the calorie consumption in the rural areas is significant (save in the 'lowest') which may be a factor for increased expenditure on food.

REFERENCE

Perspective Planning Division, *An Analysis of 1977-78 N.S.S on Energy Consumption (32nd round)*, Karnataka, Government of Karnataka, July 1981.

6

SOME ISSUES IN BIDI MANUFACTURING

Bidi Wastage

Table 6.1 presents bidi production and the proportion of wastage as reported by a typical sub-contractor during 1984-85. This Table also highlights the nature of seasonal variations in raw material supply to the bidi workers. It is seen that June and July, the peak monsoon months, report a lower raw material consumption. Excepting this, the demand for raw materials seems to be more or less uniform in other months (February excluded). Some contractors reported that during the summer months (February to May), they experienced a subdued demand for the raw materials. The month-wise production figures could be considered in the case of individual bidi-rollers (Table 6.2). Here also, the production is somewhat slack during the summer season. This Table describes how accounting is done by the individual worker as per the note book he maintains and as per the log book maintained by the contractors. Entries in the log book are usually rounded off to hundreds and reconciliation between the log book and the note book figures is done periodically or at the close of annual account. The worker has to account for the raw materials received from the contractor by rolling the stipulated quantity of bidis (usually half kg leaves and 2 0 gms of tobacco per 1000 bidis). In case he rolls a lower quantity than the stipulated rate, he has to make good for the same in his future supply to the contractor. In certain cases, it has been observed that bidi workers have to buy extra quantity of tobacco and bidi leaves to set right the deficit. The average percentage of wastage is about 4.5 as reported by the contractors (Table 6.1). According to Table 6.2, some bidi

Table 6.1 : Bidi Production and Wastage (1984-85)

Month	*Tobacco Issued (kg)*	*Bidi Leaves Issued (kg)*	*Rolled Bidi Received (mil)*	*Wastage Per cent*
November	35.0	1,100	2.0	5.0
December	40.0	1,220	2.2	4.6
January	35.0	1,100	2 0	5.0
February	28.0	1,090	1.7	4.2
March	45.0	1,400	2.5	4.0
April	38.0	1,200	2.1	4.8
May	40.0	1,300	2.3	4.4
June	29.0	1,095	1.9	4.0
July	29.0	1,090	1 8	4.0
August	40 0	2,220	2.2	4.6
September	40.0	1,300	2.3	4 4
October	40.0	1,300	2.4	4.6
Average	36.6	1,201.3	2.12	4.5

workers experienced a deficit of about 3.2 per cent which they had to make good from their pocket. Suppose if we average wage rate for rolling thousand bidis as being around Rs 13.50 (including benefits), about 3 to 5 per cent of this amount has to be deducted as going to wastage. That would mean that in a case of rolling 750 bidis per day and earning about Rs 3,600 p.a, the real wages the worker would receive after deducting for wastage, etc. may be down by 100 to 200 rupees.

A Case in Dakshina Kannada

In the Dakshina Kannada district, on an average, about Rs 1.5 crore is being collected from the bidi manufacturers as Central

Table 6.2 : Individual Production of Bidi and Accounting

Month	*As Per Log Book*	*As Per Note Book*
November	12,000	14,000
December	15,725	15,000
January	13,850	10,000
February	6,500	8,850
March	6,500	6,750
April	8,650	8,500
May	9,450	8,500
June	10,200	10,000
July	12,500	10,750
August	10,800	10,200
September	13,450	12,500
October	13,500	12,000
Total	133,125	129,050
Average	11,094	10,754
Wastage	—	3.2%

Excise duty per month since April 1984 The full-time and part-time bidi workers put together have increased to about 3 lakhs in recent months. Over 15 crore pieces of bidis are produced per day and the total wages paid amount to over Rs 20 lakhs.

There are some major bidi manufacturers like Ganesh Bidi Works, Bharath Bidi Works, P.V.S. Bidi Works and Prakash Bidi Works, who employ over two thirds of total bidi workers in the district. They have under their control over half of the total bidi contractors. Their share in the annual turnover of Rs 180 crore is quite substantial in the district. The bidis produced in this district are sent throughout the country. Bharath bidis are also exported to the Middle East countries. The exported quantity of bidis by that concern during 1980-81 was about 30 crore valued at Rs 0.51 crore. During the subsequent years (1981-82, 1982-83 and 1984-85) the quantity exported increased to over 57 crore, 75 crore and 103 crore of bidis respectively. During 1984-85, the total value of bidis exported was about Rs 2.24 crore forming a substantial proportion of exports from the country. The manpower employed by the establishment increased from 500 in 1940 to 50,000 in 1980 and gross turnover touched a figure of over Rs 22 crore. Table 6.3 describes the growth of Bharath Bidi Works from 1940 to 1980 wherein the growth seems to be quite substantial especially after 1970.

Table 6.3 : Growth of Bharath Bidi Works

Manpower	(nos)	500	3,500	11,000	20,000	50,000
Wages	(Rs cr)	0.1	0.2	0 4	1.6	6.5
Production	(cr)	2	10	16	70	115
Levys and taxes	(Rs cr)	neg	0.2	0.3	0.5	7.0
Gross turnover	(Rs cr)	0.2	0.5	1.0	5.0	22.0

Source: *Golden Jubilee Souvenir of B.B.W*, Mangalore, 1980.

Bidi Productivity Per Working and Average Day

We may note the variations in bidi productivity according to full-time and part-time bidi rolling. Table 6.4 describes monthwise working days for female and male workers and bidi productivity per working day, as well as per average day in a month. On an average, it is noticed that a female worker rolls bidis for about 25 days in a month, while a male labourer works for about 18 days. In this case, the number of working days vary from 22 in August to 28 in January for female workers.

Table 6.4 : Full-time and Part-time Bidi Production (1984-85)

(No. of bidis)

Month	*Days/worked*		*Working Prod./day*		*Prod /ave/day*	
	Female	*Male*	*Female*	*Male*	*Female*	*Male*
November	24	15	966.7	493.3	773 3	246.7
December	27	18	840.7	511.1	732.3	296.8
January	28	17	832.1	582.4	751.6	319.4
February	25	19	712.0	500.0	613.8	327.6
March	27	16	844.4	537.5	735 5	277 4
April	24	17	800.0	482.4	640.0	273.9
June	26	19	576.9	447.4	500 0	283.3
July	26	19	538.5	457.9	451 6	280.7
August	22	15	700.0	433.3	496 8	209.7
September	25	21	588.0	438.1	490 0	306.7
October	25	20	640.0	450.0	516 2	290.3
Average	25	18	713.5	485.2	610.0	283.0

For a male worker. the range is between 15 to 21 days. This is suggestive of the fact that female labourers work for a larger number of days. In cases of low production, it would be that hours worked per day would have a say as already stated. The productivity of female workers per day ranges from 538.5 bidis in July to 966.7 bidis in November. The average daily production amounts to about 731.5 bidis for the year. It is 485.2 in the case of male worker, where the variation is from 433.3 in August to 582.4 bidis in January. If we average the productivity per day in a month, the figures come to 610 for female and 283 bidis for male workers. The variation in female productivity is from 451.6 bidis in July to 773.3 bidis in November; and for male worker from 209.7 in August to 327.6 bidis in February. It is evident that for male workers, bidi-rolling is predominantly a part-time activity and as already noted, it is a low-preference occupation for them.

Bidi Labelling

Unlike bidi-rolling where "Home-working" is a common practice, labelling of bidi bundles is done in industrial premises of bidi manufacturers. The bidis are supplied to the contractors in bundles of 25. The contractors, after passing the bundles through quality control, forward the bidis to the respective manufacturers. The bundles of 25 bidis are covered with trade mark labels and 20 such bundles are packed into a bigger bundle. The average working hours for the full-time labellers is about 10 hours. The full-time workers can engage part-time workers, especially school-going children who may come and do their work during holidays and leisure time. The average wage per worker is about Rs 16.85 per day. An average worker may label about 60,000-80,000 bidis per day. The wage for labelling one lakh bidis is about Rs 23 excluding of benefits. It has been found out that bidi labelling also is a supplementary type of occupation to the family. The male workers may get the services of his children for this purpose. Some of the workers possessed small land-holding or combined labelling with agricultural labour, etc. It could be seen that children were studded in the factory and in some cases, proper ventilation and other facilities were lacking. The labourer who dries the bidis through hot air treatment is in a very unhealthy environment. Some bidi manufacturers have modern driers which reduce the drying period to less than three hours, instead of over 10 hours in traditional driers. If those manufacturers who have the traditional driers could improve the same, much labour hazards would be contained to a large extent. Like the bidi-rollers, the labellers also complain about certain health complications like asthama, T.B., etc. The workers find it difficult to avail of periodical medical check-up, fearing about fall in income. Only when there is a very severe complication that they resort to medical treatment. Owing to indifference in

Table 6.5 : Cost of Production Per 1000 Bidis

	Cost Rs	*Per cent*
Tobacco	3.00	9.2
Tendu leaves	4.00	12.3
Packing charges	0.30	0.9
Commission to contractors	1.10	3.4
Wages, salaries and benefits	14 80	45.5
Other expenses	0.60	1.8
Excise and other taxes	4.20	12.9
Manufacturers' margin	1.50	4.6
Wholesalers' margin	1.20	3.8
Retailers' margin	1.80	5.6
Total cost	32.50	100 0

Source: *Records of various bidi manufacturers*, Dakshina Kannada.

getting treatment or due to the severity of the disease, the ailment may disable the affected workers.

Because of employment of part-time child labour, children are slowly attracted to becoming full-time workers in due course and may drop out of the schools. It is not uncommon to find some children in the bidi-rolling households around bidi labelling factory.

Cost of Production

This section presents the cost of production in respect of individual bidi manufacturers in the district. Table 6.5 describes the average cost of production per thousand bidis of an average bidi manufacturer. Wages. salaries, and benefits account for about 45 per cent of the total cost. Next in importance is Central

Table 6 6 : Cost of Production Per 1000 Bidis (Prakash Bidi Works)

	Per cent
Wages	33.5
Fringe benefits	8 5
Commission to contractors	3 0
Cost of raw materials	22.0
Packing and forwarding	4 0
Other expenses	5 0
Marketing cost and margins to wholesalers and retailers	6 0
Taxes and duties	13 0
Margin to manufacturer	5.0
Total	100.0

Excise duty and other taxes (12.9 per cent). Tendu leaves and tobacco together constitute about 21.5 per cent of the cost. The margins to the contractors, manufacturers, wholesalers and retailers would largely depend upon the efficacy of the manufacturer in fixing up the margin and also according to the manipulations of all of them singly or in combination. Table 6.6 describes the cost of production per thousand bidis in the case of Prakash Bidi Works Wages, raw materials, and taxes seem to represent the average cost picture as described in Table 6.6. It is in the case of margins to wholesalers and retailers that a lower percentage is reported. But these could have been included in some form or other in cost elements like packing and forwarding and other expenses. Recently, there has been a wage increase for bidi-rollers to the extent of Rs 11.70 per 1000 bidis. Because of this increase, the bidi manufacturers have increased the wholesale and retail prices of many brands of bidis. For example, the retail prices of Ganesh bidis for a bundle of 25 which was Rs 0.95, has been increased to Rs 1.10 recently. The wholesale price has been increased to Rs 37.90 per 1000 bidis and the retail price to Rs 38.80. It could be seen that a 7 per cent increase in wage rate has induced a 15 per cent increase in retail price of bidis. Perhaps some other cost would have also increased adjunct with the labour cost.

The wage rate for rolling thousand bidis has slowly increased from Rs 4.30 in 1973 to Rs 11.70 in rate 1985. When we compare the wage rate in 1978, it was half of the rate existing in 1985.

Time and again the bidi manufacturers have been fighting for rationalisation of tax structure between branded and unbranded bidis, protection from competition from cheap cigarettes. postponement of the benefits like P.F. contributions to the bidi workers to a later date and so on. Ultimately they have to bow down before pressure and extend the benefits or contribute toward the taxes. This they would be doing by increasing the retail prices. And, as has been already noted, bidi demand has been growing very slowly and that may be a factor for the reluctance on the part of the industry to take up deep financial risks.

There have been certain legislative measures which have been beneficial to the bidi workers. It may seem that bidi manufacturers would resent excise duties and trade unions but the latter may exert pressure on the government to bring the system of bidi manufacturing under control even at the displeasure of the manufacturers. The contract system of employment came into existence in 1952 after a unworthy trial of factory system. In 1954 the government fixed the minimum wages for the bidi workers. The Bidi and Cigar Workers Act was enacted in 1966 which has been the basis for considering bidi manufacturing as an establishment. In 1974, important decisions as to bonus, holiday allowance and maternity allowance were taken. Subsequently, Bidi Workers Welfare Fund has been established to look into various welfare aspects of the bidi workers and their families.

Cooperative Bidi Industry

Owing to difficulties in procuring quality raw materials and also due to the exploitative nature of bidi manufacturers, co-operative movement among bidi-rollers was started in early sixties. Kerala has been one of the earliest to start Bidi Workers' Industrial Cooperative Societies. When trade union activities were at the helm of affairs, it became unprofitable for the manufacturers of certain bidi brands to produce bidis and they resorted to labour-cut. Once the volatile trade unionists were removed, the other workers with the encouragement of government started cooperative societies among themselves. In Kerala, the Kerala Dinesh Bidi Workers Central Society with about 22 primary societies attached to it is in the cooperative sector. It markets the bidis under the brand name 'Dinesh Bidis'. The total number of members which was small in the beginning has grown up to 40,000 in recent times. Each primary society on an average produces about 4 cr of bidis per year and employs about 1800 workers.

Bidi-rolling in the cooperative sector is done in the industrial premises as against "home-working" in the private sector. The wage rates are slightly higher in the case of the cooperative bidi workers. An incentive form of dearness allowance is paid when the worker rolls over a certain quantity of bidis per day. While the basic wage rate is Rs 12 per thousand bidis, the D.A amounts to Rs 3.60 per thousand if the workers produces more than 800 bidis per day. If the individual production is less than that, the worker does not get the D.A. Henec, this incentive might induce the workers to produce the stipulated quantity of bidis to get entitled for a better wage rate. The working hours are normally from 8.30 in the morning to 6.00 in the evening. That would mean that a bidi-roller should produce a minimum of 80 bidis per hour if he wants to benefit from the incentive. It could be seen that in "Home-working", the average number of bidis rolled per hour has been 75 in the rural area and 71 in the semi-urban area in the case of female workers. For male workers, the average has been higher by about 10 per cent. So. it should be possible for the cooperative workers to produce the stipulated quantity of bidis per day to get the maximum benefit. It is found that in the cooperative sector also, about 80 per cent of workers are female members.

Unlike the private sector where the bonus rate is 8.33 per cent, bonus for the cooperative worker is distributed according to profits. For example, it is not uncommon to find a bonus rate of 11.75 per cent being paid to the workers of the Manjeshwar Bidi Workers' Industrial Cooperative Society in Kasargod district. There has been no difference in provident fund contribution which has been fixed at 6.25 per cent. Every member is entitled to a medical allowance of Rs 30 per year. Every Sunday is a paid holiday, besides eight festival holidays. The members are entitled to one day paid holiday per 20 working days. Female workers are entitled to three months maternity leave up to the second issue as in the private sector. The maternity allowance amounts to Rs 400 and in the private sector, it ranges between Rs 300 and Rs 400 depending on the quantity of work done by the members prior to taking the leave. From the death relief fund, an amount of Rs 5000 is given to the family of the deceased worker. For this, every member has to pay a minimum contribution of Rs 12 per year. If the worker completes 12 or more years of service, he is entitled to a retirement benefit of Rs 3000 as per the Retirement Benefit Scheme. For this also, each member has to contribute Rs 12 per year. If the worker leaves the society before the 12th year, the contribution is not refunded and is kept in the R B S. The workers have a thrift fund and they can take interest-free loans from that. They are entitled festival advance also from the societies.

All these suggest that the conditions of cooperative bidi workers is comparatively better than the "home-workers". But they have a less degree of flexibility and for the cooperative societies the major problem has been huge wage bill.

Table 6.7 describes the cost of production per thousand bidis in the cooperative sector wherein wages and salaries account for over 55 per cent of the total cost of production. In this case, the society enjoys a profit of about 10 per cent. The primary societies sell the produce to the central society at Cannanore at Rs 33.50 per thousand bidis. They may get a share of certain proportion of the profit from the central society as commission and at times it ranges up to 20 per cent. The cooperative societies are under the supervision of the district industrial department. The Deputy Director of Industries is also the Registrar of the industrial cooperative societies. The societies are governed by the bye-laws and have elected representatives who look after the day-to-day affairs of the societies A major problem in the functioning of the societies has been difficulties encountered in the procurement of quality raw materials on time. Also, it is reported that some societies

Table 6.7 : Cost of Production Per 1000 Bidis in the Cooperative Sector

Sl No.	*Item*	*Rs P*	*Per cent*
	Bidi leaves	4.22	13.7
	Bidi tobacco	1.82	5.9
	Packing charges	0.77	2 5
	Wages and salaries	17.05	55.5
	Excise duty	3.84	12.5
	Other expenses	3.03	9.9
	Total	30.73	100.0
	Sale price to head office	33.50	

Source: The Manjeshwar Bidi Workers' Industrial Cooperative Society Ltd.

owe a huge amount of dues to the raw materials suppliers. The Kerala government is providing a certain proportion of subsidy depending on the quantity of production by the societies. It could be seen that because the cooperative societies are facing certain peculiar problems, the system is not spreading to other areas.

REFERENCES

Indian Tobacco Journal, Vol. 16, Nos 3 and 4, 1984-85.

"The Kerala Dinesh Bidi Workers Central Society Ltd. records."

Memoranda submitted by the "Karnataka Bidi Industry Association", (Regd.) and All India Bidi Manufacturers Federation Ltd.. Bombay.

Golden Jubilee Souvenir of Bharath Bidi Works P. Ltd. Mangalore, 1980.

7

RELATIONSHIP BETWEEN INCOME AND OTHER VARIABLES

An attempt is made to relate standard per capita income to expenditure, saving, borrowing and asset pattern of the bidi households (Table 7.1). It appears in certain cases that per capita total expenditure is higher than per capita income. In Ullal this is evident in groups III, IV and VII where per capita expenditure is higher by about 40 per cent (group IV) to 4 per cent (group III). In Pajir also, per capita expenditure is higher than per capita income in groups VI, VII and VIII. The difference is quite substantial in the last group. Because of this feature in the full-time bidi households, it is found that the group average expenditure is more than the group average income. The average expenditure in Pajir for the entire sample is also higher than the average income.

In Pajir full-time households, a larger proportion of male population has been reported as unemployed. It should be presumed that atleast a certain proportion of this would have sought employment elsewhere which has not been reported. Hence, while considering the income and expenditure pattern of Pajir full-time households, the fact that unemployment rate is quite high has to be properly reckoned with, because the corresponding average borrowing position does not show any appreciable increase in the particular cases. It seems that the gap in such cases is left uncovered for years together The average per capita borrowing is Rs 331 for Pajir full-timers,

Table 7.1 : Per Capita Income, Expenditure, Asset and Saving Patterns (Rs/p.a)

Size Group	Stand Income U	Stand Income P	Stand Expendi U	Stand Expendi P	Savings U	Savings P	Loons U	Loons P	Assets U	Assets P	Savings Rate % U	Savings Rate % P
I	2084	1385	1912	1235	41	25	336	110	834	287	2.0	2.0
II	1934	1674	1638	1431	42	102	81	486	856	228	2.0	5.8
III	1564	1962	1640	1211	250	49	150	97	332	217	15.3	1.6
IV	1275	1840	1808	1807	47	61	299	155	698	436	2.4	3.4
Sub-ave.	1940	1679	1768	1464	67	64	216	245	770	302	3.3	3.9
V	2167	1572	2069	1441	279	126	385	269	251	241	11.7	7.8
VI	1520	1674	1445	1697	78	74	172	208	248	256	4.3	5.2
VII	1139	1215	1316	1387	52	61	45	840	187	575	4.1	4.3
VIII	1673	987	1419	1615	68	165	248	214	288	365	5.0	15.7
Sub-ave.	1673	1320	1576	1538	122	127	233	331	253	320	7.2	9.3
Average	1862	1463	1713	1510	83	103	221	299	620	314	4.3	7.0

U=Ullal ; P=Pajir

where it is slightly lower for the part-timers (Rs 245). Actually group VII report a high borrowing rate when compared to others. Therefore, the gap between expenditure and income has to be bridged through other variables like unemployment, under-productivity and under-reporting.

There is not much difference in the savings rate except in some groups (III and V in Ullal and V and VIII in Pajir). The savings rate is quite high in these size groups. The average savings rate is 4.3 per cent in Ullal; for the full-timers it is 7.2 per cent. Curiously enough, the part-timers, whose average

Table 7.2 : Part-time and Full-time Units : An Evaluation

Variables	*ULLAL*		*PAJIR*	
	Part-time	*Full-time*	*Part-time*	*Full-time*
Family size (per h/h)	6.6	5.1	6.1	6.2
Working hours (day)	8.9	9.6	8.5	9.1
Labour Productivity (bidis/day)	603.4	713.6	620.5	692.3
Per worker bidi income (Rs)	1,939	2,630	1,772	2,056
Per worker total income (Rs)	3,178	2,949	2,287	2,012
Per capita income (Rs)	1,941	1,673	1,679	1,330
Per capita expenditure (Rs)	1,768	1,576	1,464	1,538
Per capita food expend. (Rs)	1,003	898	1,062	1,117
Per capita education expend. (Rs)	24.1	19.0	14.6	24.6
Per capita health expend. (Rs)	141.1	80.9	93.0	110.8
Per capita fuel expend. (Rs)	141.9	180.8	47.3	43.4
Per capita savings rate (%)	3.3	7.2	3.9	9.3

income is higher. have a lower savings rate (3.3 per cent). In Pajir also, full-timers report a higher savings rate. For the entire sample, the savings rate is comparatively higher in Pajir. It should be noted that per capita food expenditure forms a considerable proportion of total expenditure in Pajir. The contention that the full-time households spend more on food there, does not preclude the savings rate to be smaller. Though the bulk of savings is in the shape of provident fund contributions, some households have additional savings also. Regular saving through chit funds and related means seems to be a common feature noticed in such high saving cases.

As already noted, the asset position does not include investment in buildings, jewellery or livestock. The per capita asset holding is Rs 620 in Ullal and Rs 314 in Pajir. The Ullal full-timers have a very low asset holding (Rs 253) than the part-timers (Rs 770). This has to be contrasted with the high savings rate existing in the full-time units. In Pajir however, the per capita asset holding is slightly higher in full-time units (Rs 320 as against Rs 302 in part-time units). The ralationship between all these variables has been illustrated in Table 7.2 in a summary form.

In Ullal, it seems that a larger family size with lower working hours in part-time units result in lower bidi productivity and income when compared to the full-time units. However, the total income is slightly higher and also the per capita standard income. The per capita expenditure is higher in this category which higher expenditure on food, health and education. The full-time units report a higher bidi productivity and a lower per capita expenditure, except in fuel consumption. The savings rate in their case is higher.

In Pajir, the family size is more or less similar and the part-time units report slightly lower working hours per day and also bidi productivity like the Ullal samples, Here, total income is higher with lower per capita expenditure. Expenditure on food, health and education is higher in full-time units and in fuel consumption there is not much difference. The savings rate is higher in full-time units, though they have a higher per capita expenditure.

Two interesting things are evident from the above analysis. In the semi-urban sample, the part-time bidi households seem to have a higher bidi income and productivity. But the full-time households have a better consumption pattern and higher savings rate. Though the full-time units have a higher savings rate in Pajir also, the part-time units perform efficiently in consumption expenditure as well as bidi productivity. Therefore, the rural part-time units, if they are induced toward a higher savings rate, can perform efficiently than what they are now. This would suggest that bidi-rolling, if supplemented with other activities, might have a higher productivity and employment structure.

Food Consumption

A major issue pertaining to full-time bidi households in the semi-urban area is lower per capita calorie consumption per day. In the rural sample, however, the full-timers enjoy above-average food consumption standard. Nutrition problem, therefore, is prominent in the former cases, though not a severe one. The standardised calorie level (1867 K.cal/day) is lower and especially in groups VII and VIII, the average seems to be very poor. These two groups report lower per capita food expenditure than others. Curiously enough, they report a lower standard for other expenditure also. Group VII reports relatively a higher expenditure pattern in fuel consumption. The standard per capita income is very low in group VII and expenditure there, higher than the income. If expenditure were to be lower than income, the severity of nutrition problem would have been greater. Group VII, however, reports a higher per capita income than expenditure and in this case, the per capita food consumption level could be slightly increased. Incidentally, in this group, the calorie consumption averaged is the lowest at 1612.8 K.cal/day.

The part-timers have a moderate level of food energy consumption and in Pajir, both types of households report high calorie consumption (excepting group I, where it is only 1746.7 K.cal/day). Since a low level of food expenditure may have related health problems, especially in a coastal area such as Ullal, proper health care, coupled with adequate nutrition has to be safeguarded for the bidi-workers who have to work under unfavourable conditions. Here, the ills of drinking may be mentioned.

Conditions of Bidi Labour

From the analysis it has been observed that bidi labourers have to work for about 9 hours a day which is average for any other occupation in the semi-urban or rural areas. It should be noted that these 9 hours are not utilised continuously. Bidi productivity increases with the increase in the share of bidi income to total income. Though per worker bidi income is high in a semi-urban area for the full-timers, the per capita total income is lower in their case. This is mainly due to the fact that bidi labour is not that remunerative as other seasonal activities in the given region. The full-time bidi-rollers have a better expenditure pattern and a higher savings rate.

In Ullal, of the 52 bidi households interviewed, four have a per capita income of less than Rs 1100 p.a. In two of these cases, complete production figures were not made available owing to certain reasons like death of a member, etc. In the other two cases, the family size is above the average. A norm of Rs 1100 has been taken to determine the minimum economic position of a bidi household. In the integrated rural development programmes, a norm of Rs 700 per capita is taken to determine the poverty line. Since this figure refers to 1978-79, for the current year the break-even figure should be more than Rs 1000 per capita. On this basis, it may not be possible to suggest inclusion of some bidi workers under the I.R.D. programme. From the viewpoint of expenditure also, no family in the sample should be termed as very poor since the per capita standard expenditure is more or less similar to that of income.

In Pajir, however, some full-time bidi households (about 12 per cent of the total) seem to have less than Rs 1000 per capita income per year. The norm of Rs 1000 has been taken for rural areas keeping the comparatively self-sustaining nature there in agricultural production, etc. But even in these cases, if the per capita expenditure is considered, no household seems to fall below the poverty line, since the expenditure is more than the income. However, it can be visualised that if these families are included, under the I.R.D. programme, their income-expenditure position could become favourable because of asset-push. Though we feel that bidi labourers as such require little government assistance for subsidies, etc. when compared to the other poor labourers, it should be worth-trying if some large families, where the per capita income is lower (especially when compared to expenditure) could be taken up for assistance in one or other form.

The Feasibility of Cooperative Movement

The working of the cooperative bidi societies in Kerala state has been highlighted earlier. It has been observed that workers get a larger benefit rate and other incentives. If they produce more, they get a higher bonus rate also. Their interests are protected by the society and the government since they are organised as industrial workers like in any other organised sector.

We may try to see whether the system of cooperative bidi manufacturing could be tried in the Dakshina Kannada district. In this district, bidi workers get a higher wage rate than in many others states (excluding Kerala). The manufacturers seem to provide the necessary minimum wage rates and other benefits to the bidi workers. Of course, when compared to the cooperative bidi workers in Kerala, bidi workers in this district may get about 25 per cent less wages, provided that the bidi workers in Kerala produce a minimum of 800 bidis per day. But according to the performance of a society, it has been found that the per capita daily production of bidis is about 640, which would reduce the wages of the cooperative workers by more than 20 per cent. From our own study, it has been noticed that the per capita production is not more than 700 per day. So disallowing for the D.A incentive, the net benefit a cooperative worker might get would be only marginal. But employment security and absence of exploitation prevail for the cooperative worker.

A great disadvantage would be the lack of flexibility in attending to householdc hores. If the "home-workers" were to be organised into cooperative societies, investment in industrial premises, buildings, procurement of raw materials, etc. might result in a huge capital-rush. No doubt, a certain proportion of the manufacturers and many contractors may exploit the illiterate and non-union members to a large extent to get the maximum profit. Also, there has been competition from the unbranded and duplicate bidis which might indirectly check the exploitative nature of manufactures of branded bidis. In order to maintain a steady market, they will have to keep the bidi workers in good terms by providing them the basic benefits and also by maintaining the quality of bidis. In some cases, the exploitative nature of the sub-contractors has been noticed. In Pajir, most of the sub-contractors have their own provision shops and the bidi workers are encouraged to solicit them. The wages to be paid are adjusted towards the provisions they buy. Some contractors deliberately reduce the number of bidis rolled by some or many members in their log books submitted to the principal employers. That means that though some workers would get the basic wage rate for the bidis they roll, they may stand to lose a certain proportion of benefits legitimate to them. The sub-contractors may also stipulate a higher bidi turnover for given quantity of bidi leaves and tobacco and in case of deficits, may cut a sizeable proportion as wastage besides accounting a lower production figure.

It has also been noticed that some contractors would not register some workers and may exploit the fringe benefits accruable in such cases to their own advantage. Lack of active participation in union activities, non-unionisation, indifference, allegiance to particular contractors owing to tradition or indebtedness, have been some of the factors for the plight of bidi workers. It is these workers who want no intermediaries between themselves and the manufacturers. If some type of cooperation is prevailed upon them, that may enable them to reach the manufacturer directly and get the benefits. Majority of the workers have little complaint against the manufacturers as such.

It is common to hear complaints from the manufacturers also since most of the private industrialists are weary of the government tax policy and labour problems. Increased cost of production and thereby increasing the bidi prices might even cut down the bidi demand to a certain extent, especially when pitted against cheap cigarettes and unbranded and duplicate bidis. Perhaps the best policy could be in strictly enforcing the tax rates in all the cases, supervision of the contractors, and especially the sub-contractors, periodically checking of the wage and benefit accounts and encouraging bidi exports. Every year, inflation-based wage increase could keep the living conditions of the workers stable. In the procurement and transport of raw materials, a likewise policy should be adopted wherein much cost and time could be saved.

Rural Development

The Integrated Rural Development Programme has been in operation since October 1980 in this district. The strategy was slightly modified during 1982-83 to select projects of the borrowers according to their ability and repayment capacity. Up to 1984-85, a total number of 29,290 beneficiaries were covered under the programme. In this, the Scheduled Castes and Scheduled Tribes and women were beneficiaries. The total loan amount disbursed during these five years was Rs 7.35 crore and subsidy. another Rs 2.83 crore.

Dakshina Kannada district ranks as one of the foremost districts in the state in socio-economic conditions. For a population of about 2.5 million, the total number of units benefited so far under the government programmes would hardly amount to about 6.0 per cent. But then with the limited resources available under the programme, it could be said that its critical evaluation in this district would have a low profile unlike at the national level, where there has been much debate on its effectiveness.

Recently, from a re-survey of the I R.D.P. beneficiaries in the district, it has been found out that about 25 per cent of people live below the poverty line, i.e. below Rs 3500 per annum per household of 5 members. When one compares this with the national or state average of about 40 per cent or more, one could get an awareness of the better economic development in the district.

But even in this district, there have been cases of misutilization of funds and occurrence of asset-perish. In a survey of about 4249 assets covering animal husbandry, it was noted that about 72 per cent of the created assets still existed and were found to be useful. About 20 per cent of the assets were missing (about 71 per cent of the animals were reported to have died and the rest either sold out or left with other parties). The rest of the assets (8 per cent) were either partly used or of no use. Deliberate misuse was observed in as many as 250 cases (about 6 per cent of total assets). It also noted that, of the total 613 animals dead, 379 belonged to landless labourers. 214 to marginal farmers and 20 to small farmers. The proportion of sold out animals was also very high in the first two cases. This shows how problematic it is for the landless labourers and marginal farmers (to a certain extent) in maintaining animal husbandry (milch cattle) assets.

As regards loan repayment, 80 per cent of the cases have already started repayment. The overall finding of the government survey has been that about 32 per cent of the units have been substantially benefited and about 50 per cent partially benefited. According to 1985-86 annual action plan of the district, re-covering a substantial proportion of beneficiaries who have not been benefited by earlier plans, has been taken up during this year, especially in the livestock sector.

Rural development involves restructuring and development of all the rural sectors—agriculture, horticulture, animal husbandry, fisheries, rural industries and transport and establishments. Since government cannot handle this mighty task (even in this, owing to cases of ineffectiveness), sooner or later, the bulk of the burden of assisting the sectors would fall on the private enterprises and the rural population at large.

REFERENCES

District Rural Development Society, *Annual Action Plan for 1985-86*, Mangalore, Dakshina Kannada, 1985.

District Rural Development Society, 'I R D P Asset verification in Dakshina Kannada District', Mangalore (mimeo), 1985.

Syndicate Bank. *Annual Action Plan 1984 for Dakshina Kannada District*, Lead Bank Section, Mangalore, 1984.

Syndicate Bank, *Annual Action Plan 1985 for Dakshina Kannada District*, Lead Bank Section, Mangalore, 1985.

8

THE IMPACT OF BIDI-ROLLING ON FEMALE-HEADED HOUSEHOLDS

Introduction

An attempt has been made to study the impact of bidi-rolling in female-headed households. For this purpose, a sample of 10 households where females were the heads of the household were selected in Ullal. This is in addition to an equal number of samples covered in the case of male-headed households. Particulars covering working conditions, income generation, expenditure pattern, decision-making capacity in major household and work variables, health and sanitation, etc. have been included for the study. A major departure from the main study is with relation to decision-making capacity of the female heads.

Decision-making

Decision-making is a process wherein different members of the household take part actively or passively about family maintenance, working conditions, asset creation, new ventures, nature of expenditure, social relations, etc. Table 8.1 describes the role played by the female heads of bidi households in deciding the course of various operations and activities to be undertaken by the family members. Female heads take major decisions on family maintenance, how the income has to be expended, education of children, celeberation of festivals, and recreation. They take an equal part in deciding the nature of working conditions, asset creation, engagement of workers, repairs and construction, work seeking, and health. When compared to the male-headed bidi households, the decision analysis is equally spread over different aspects. In male-headed households, decision on important matters are concentrated in the male head, whereas in the female-headed households, other members have also a say in the important aspects of the family.

Table 8.1 : Decision-Making Capacity of Female Heads

Activity	*(Proportion of Participation)* *Major*	*Equal*	*Minor*	*Nil*
Asset creation	0.30	0.50	0.10	0.10
Working conditions	0.35	0 35	—	0.30
Family maintenance	0.50	0 30	—	0 20
Expenditure	0.33	0.52	—	0.15
Work-seeking	0.30	0.30	0.10	0.30
Engagement of workers	0.30	0.50	0 10	0 10
Health	0 28	0.48	0 24	—
Education	0 37	0 33	—	0.30
Social relations	0.12	0.50	—	0.38
Festivals	0.25	0.50	0.25	—
Recreation	0 25	0 35	0.30	0.10
New ventures	0.23	0.32	0.20	0 25
Repairs and construction	0.25	0.40	0.10	0.25
Travel	0.25	0.25	0.10	0.40
Overall	0.30	0 41	0.08	0.21

Taken the nature of decision-making process of the households it seems that female household heads take major or equal role in decision-making in about 71.0 per cent cases. Taking decisions on equal basis with other family members is more intensive than being the major decision maker. In about 8.0 per cent cases, the female heads play a minor role and in 21.0

per cent of the cases, their role is practically nil. As contrasted to this, in the male-headed households, females played an equal role in about 40.0 per cent of the cases but their major role was very low at about 12.0 per cent only. Their major role was substantial in cases like asset creation, family maintenance and social relations. It is interesting to note that in both female

Table 8.2 : Sources of Income for Bidi Households

	Female-headed H/H (Rs per H/H)	*Male-headed H/H (Rs per H/H)*
Self income—Permanent	3,120	2,983
—Temporary	—	—
Female income—Permanent	3,120	1,800
—Temporary	—	—
Male income—Permanent	4,640	4,960
—Temporary	4,190	4,800
Total income—Permanent	10,880	7,943
—Temporary	4,190	6,600
Total household income/p.a	15,070	14,543
Per capita income	2,319	2,424

and male-headed households, other males and females including aged children play decisive roles in taking family decisions. It would be profitable to compare certain variables between the 2 types of households to bring out the salient differences.

Working Conditions

In the sample households, 68.8 per cent of female heads were illiterates while the proportion for male and children were 28.6 and 5 0 per cent respectively. The average family size was 6.8, females and males 2.5 each and children 1.8. The average number of family workers was 3.6-1.8 femalses, 1.0 males and 0.2 children. Besides bidi-rolling, some other members were looking after other subsidiary occupations also. Some temporary callings were sought by some of the male members. The average working hours per day was about 8.6 hours for all the members including bidi-rollers. The average working hours, however, were higher in bidi-rolling as such by about 10 to 15 per cent. In bidi-rolling, cutting of bidi leaves and tobacco consumed about 40.0 per cent of total bidi labour, rolling of bidi sharing about 44.0 per cent. Bundling, transport and miscellaneous operations shared the rest. Though one weekly holiday was allowable for the bidi workers, very few availed of this facility Some of the female respondents reported of working even up to 11 hours a day in bidi making.

Apart from wage earning, female members and also a certain proportion of child and male labour were engaged in domestic work. This would include cooking, serving, washing and cleaning, water fetching, fuel gathering, shopping, house maintenance and other activities. Cooking and serving consumed about 3.9 hours per day of which the contribution of self labour was about 60.0 per cent. Washing and cleaning and water fetching consumed about 2 hours and the share of self labour in this was about 45.0 per cent. Fuel gathering on an average consumed about 0.3 hours and shopping about 0.6 hours. In this also, the contribution of self labour was about 50 to 60 per cent. All these activities required about 7 to 8 hours of family labour per day. Time spent on water fetching, fuel gathering and shopping varied between the households depending upon type of labour, locality and availability of facilities.

Self and Family Income

An attempt has been made to compare self (respondent's) and total family income from permanent and temporary sources of employment (including bidi-rolling) for female as well as male members. Table 8.2 describes different sources of income in the female and male-headed households for self, other female and males. The pattern of annual household income suggests that bidi-rolling was being treated by the workers as giving a permanent source of income. The female respondents including other females added Rs 3120 as permanent income. The male members contributed Rs 4640 as permanent income and Rs 4190 as temporary income. The total household income worked out to Rs 15,070 with per capita income of Rs 2,319 in the female-headed households. In the male-headed households self income (i.e. income of the female respondents) was lower, whereas male income was substantial. The reason for this was due to a larger proportion of male workers. Though the household income was lower in this case, the per capita income was slightly higher than that existing for the female-headed households.

The pattern of expenditure between the households showed that female-headed households spent a lower proportion on food, beverages, education, entertainment and travel, while in the male headed households, expenditure on food and beverages was significant. Food was the major item of expenditure in both the households accounting for 69.7 per cent in the former and 73.3 per cent in the latter cases. Significant is to note a sizeable portion of expenditure on cosmetics, entertainment, rituals, etc. Besides, beverages, clothing, travel and especially fuel account for significant share of the household expenditure. The saving ratio is 6.9 per cent for the female-headed households and 6.0 per cent for the male-headed households (Table 8.3).

Socio-Economic Conditions

It was observed that about 20.0 per cent of the female heads were indifferent to their husbands or other males and in turn they reported that their husbands were indifferent towards them in about 33.0 per cent of the cases. The indifference towards children and other females was greater. About 23.0 per cent of the female heads had good opinion about their neighbours. About 12.5 per cent of the households had joint family system. About 50.0 per cent of the cases were aware of local politics and about 10.0 per cent about outside politics also. 26.0 per cent of the heads were actively involved in social and voluntary services and 10.0 per cent were members in local organisations.

About 40 0 per cent of the families lived in kutcha houses and 20 0 per cent of the houses had less than 2 rooms. 28.0 per cent of the households depended upon common wells for drinking water facilities. About 60.0 per cent of the houses had wells in their compounds. Ventilation facilities were very poor and also sanitation which proved to be hazardous to the bidi-rollers. Some chronic diseases were common amongst them, more so in the case of male bidi-rollers. About 10.0 per cent

Table 8.3 : Expenditure Pattern in the Female/ Male Household (%)

Particulars	*Female-headed H/Hs*	*Male-headed H/Hs*
Food items	69.7	73.3
Beverages	5 6	6.6
Clothing	3.8	3.0
Cosmetics	0 6	0.5
Utencils	1.5	1.2
Health	1.7	1 6
Education	0.4	0.7
Fuel	5.2	5.3
Entertainment	1.7	2.0
Travel	2.0	2.5
Rituals	0.3	0.3
Others	9.0	3.0
Total h/h expenditure (Rs)	14,030	13,670
Per capita expenditure (Rs)	2,159	2,278
Savings ratio	6.9	6.0

of the households reported severe health problems and about 25 0 per cent mild problems. In a few cases, the diseases were chronic and disabled the workers such that they could not undertake any other work other than bidi-rolling. These particulars were found to be similar in male-headed households also.

It has been observed that the productivity of bidi labour was slightly higher in the female-headed households due to longer working hours. The rate of involvement of child labour in bidi-rolling and labelling was higher in these cases. It was observed that in certain cases, male members smoked off a sizeable quantity of bidis that they rolled. This aspect put them in ever deficit with the contractors who would debit to their account the difference in actual and should-be production. Bidi-rolling in the area supplemented income from agriculture and services and helped in improving the productive base of the families. In certain cases, petty shop owners not only rolled bidis but acted as sub-contractors also. This peculiar multi-activity enterprise was highly paying to them. This is a clear indication of the direction that some of the rural programmes could aim at.

9

DIVERSIFICATION AND INTEGRATION

Rural Development is best achieved with decentralised diversification of activities and at the same time effecting a workable integration among them. In many of the rural programmes, this aspect has been amptly emphasized but due to divergences in priorities, coordination, etc. very little has been achieved in this regard. We may consider the nature of diversification of various activities resulting from bidi-rolling and how spontaneous integration is being attempted in this case.

Tobacco is being used for manufacture of bidi, chewing tobacco, cigar and cheroot, cigarettes, hookha, jarda, scented tobacco, snuff, extracts and essences and others. During the period 1960-61 to 1983-84. area under tobacco in the country increased at an annual growth rate of 0.44 per cent, while production increase was at 2.19 per cent. Productivity increased at 1.75 per cent per annum. Andhra Pradesh and Gujarat accounted for 78.1 per cent of the tobacco area in the country followed by Karnataka whose share has been about 6 0 per cent. Other states (Bihar, Maharashtra, Orissa, Tamil Nadu, Uttar Pradesh, West Bengal) accounted for the balance. In the major tobacco producing states, the growth rates in area, production and productivity has been positive, especially in Gujarat and Karnataka followed by Andhra Pradesh. The other states reported negative growth rates notably in area and production. The variability in tobacco production was found higher in the case of states having higher growth rates in production. Production variability rises from uncertain weather conditions, diseases and pests, resource constraints, technological change and price fluctuations.

Cultivation of bidi tobacco is labour intensive, demanding periodical interculture, weeding, topping, desuckering, stalk cutting, sun curing, ploughing land after stalk cutting and removal of stumps. Karnataka has an area of over 25,000 ha. under bidi tobacco, besides other tobacco varieties. Cultivation of bidi tobacco is concentrated in Belgaum, Bellary and Mysore districts. Of the total cost of cultivation, curing consumes about 51.0 per cent. The other important items of expenditure are fertilisers, labour, overhead cost, nursery, farmyard manure and pesticides in order of importance. The average yield of uncured tobacco is about 12 tonnes per ha. After curing in the barns, the yield of the finished product comes to about 1.2 tonnes.

Smoking quality is the major consideration in the quality of bidi tobacco. The physical characteristics valued are colour, texture intensity of spangling and degree of granulation. The tobacco growers have problems of processing, marketing and others. Assistance in installing tobacco curing barns and marketing facilities would be advantageous to them. For the bidi-rollers, quality of tendu leaves and tobacco are very important in order to turn out quality produce. Owing to lack of storage facilities and transportation bottlenecks, the quality of raw materials are impaired. Hence, improvements in these spheres would integrate bidi manufacturing toward better quality, standards and markets.

Every year about 2,43,000 mt of manufactured and unmanufactured tobacco is being exported from India. Of this, bidis and unmanufactured tobacco for manufacture of bidi exported is quite low (0.4 per cent) and hence improvement of bidi tobacco would go a long way in mitigating the problems of growers, bidi rollers and other workers involved in that and improve the export potentiality.

It is believed that statistical association between smoking and cancer is well-established but the cause and effect relationship might not be. The data from various sources has been examined and it is found that the claim that smoking causes lung cancer or coronary heart diseases is not established and rests on inadequate evidence. The issue of passive smoking is also proved to be a low health-hazard. We will have to view the role tobacco plays in the economies of many countries in terms of income, employment, tax revenue and foreign exchange it yields with proper perspective.

It may seem that too many restrictions on tobacco trade will harm the growth potential of this sector in many countries. In view of this economic importance, it is a must that this particular sector is given its due importance. Starting from growers to the consumers, bidi manufacturing involves many stages. The areas where tobacco cultivation is concentrated may not possess the necessary infrastructure facilities for manufacture of bidi and other tobacco products. Tradition, availability of labour and trade facilities which are specialised in bidi-rolling and government policy are some of the factors responsible for growth of bidi industry. Mangalore in Karnataka is considered to be the bidi capital of India. From this place, bidi is being exported to other countries also. Recently, export of king-sized bidis has commenced. Besides branded bidis, unbranded bidis are also manufactured by many bidi households. It is found that the quality of the unbranded bidis is very satisfactory but due to lack of proper marketing facilities, the same is not being encouraged. It is a matter of concern that duplicate and spurious brands of bidis are also marketed causing hardships to the genuine bidi makers and consumers. Rationalisation of tax, checking the circulation of duplicate bidis and encouragement of quality unbranded bidis, besides effecting efficiency in storage and transport of raw materials could be factors in the proper integration of the different stages in bidi manufacturing. After all, the purpose of integration is to further develop the particular system.

In rural development, integration plays a very important role. Integration between objectives, agencies, areas and different sectors is essential to realise the optimal use of human and physical resources and improving system efficiency at all levels. For this, proper identification, effective coordination and efficiency in the delivery system, etc. become paramount. It could be argued that if the existing facilities are better used in the given sectors, that particular situation would prove to be more profitable than creating new ones. The recent rural development projects emphasise more on the latter aspect. Improvement of sectors which have high growth potential should also be incorportated into the institutional set-up. The excessive importance given to the primary sector has resulted in neglect of the secondary and the tertiary sectors, at the same time not improving the efficiency in the primary sector. Bidi-rolling being an important activity in rural areas should be covered under special programmes for development. This applies to other sectors as well requiring encouragement and development initiatives.

Without development initiatives the concerned sector may not grow in the desired level and the top-sided growth would impair workable integration. With proper incentives, the process could be made more progressive and specialisation of activities would lead to diversification. When all the sub-sectors are developing, integration among them would be a feasible achievement. The rural programmes have to fall back on this premise and suitably amend their approaches so as to accommodate not only relief measures throughout the regions with due consideration of area specifications, etc. but also problem sectors which require the development initiatives.

REFERENCES

Economic Research Department, "Evaluation of a NABARD-Refinanced Scheme of Financing Tobacco Barns Implemented by the Virajpet Branch of the State Bank of India in Coorg District, Karnataka", State Bank of India, Bombay, 1984.

R.H. Patel et al., "Trends and Variability in Area, Production and Productivity of Tobacco in India", *Indian Tobacco Journal*, XVIII : October-December 1986.

A.N. Singh et al., "The Production, Marketing and Manufacture of Tobacco and Tobacco Products in Karnataka", *Indian Tobacco Journal*, XII : July-September 1980.

R.D. Tollison (ed.), *Smoking and Society : Toward a More Balanced Assessment*, Lexington Books, D.C. Heath and Co., Massachusettes, 1985.

10

CONCLUSIONS

Summary

Rural development has been viewed in a narrow sense so as to include only the poorest of the poor of the rural economy. Simply giving cash subsidies where asset-creation capacity or specific infrastructural facilities are lacking would prove a heavy drain on the resources of the economy. It should be viewed that after all there are better avenues for optimal utilisation of resources. In this regard, it may said that development of specialised sectors like bidi-rolling might prove doubly advantageous in that it would create assets among the poor bidi-rollers, at the same time developing that sector. This need not mean that the existing approach of rural programmes be abandoned and emphasis given more on the non-poor. It is a question of proper policy mix and identification of the problem issues. Scarce resources have to be utilised fully and diversification of the impact of the programmes is the answer. Theoretically speaking, rural development aims at diversification of the rural sector and integration of the different sub-sectors toward an optimal system efficiency. Since this aspect is lacking in practice, it is high time that they are energised so as to prove as real development initiatives in the process of reconstruction.

With this viewpoint, an attempt has been made to study a particular developing rural sub-sector like bidi-rolling and consider various aspects of bidi-labour and how their problems could be mitigated. In this respect, the study aims at a partial rural development. There could be other sub-sectors which also demand specialised treatment so as to evolve a complete process.

Dakshina Kannada district accounts for about 8 per cent of total bidi labour in the country and is a major bidi concentrated region. A study was undertaken to evaluate the labour conditions of bidi workers in the district, with respect to their working conditions, production capacity, consumption patterns and standard of living. The analysis has been attempted in the case of full-time and part-time labour in rural and semi-urban climates in the Mangalore and Bantwal taluks of the district.

The first chapter presents a general description about bidi industry in the country—production estimates, cost of production and other particulars. The second chapter lists the objectives of the study and how the field survey was conducted; the next chapter highlights labour distribution—male, female and child in the sample areas according to full-time (where over 60 per cent of total household income is obtained through bidi-rolling) and part-time bidi households. Of the 34 part-time and 18 full-time households in Ullal in Mangalore taluk (semi-urban area) and 17 part-time and 27 full-time households in Pajir in Bantwal taluk (a rural area) covered, the average number of bidi workers was 1.67 and 1.88 in the part-time and 2.14 and 2.52 in the full-time households. Female workers constituted over 82.0 per cent in both the semi-urban and rural areas, participation of male and child labour was rather supplementary. In the semi-urban area, the average number of workdays was 240.6 for male (slightly higher under part-time), 235.6 for female (slightly higher under full-time) and 236.5 for child labour (slightly higher under full-time).

In the rural area, the average workdays were slightly lower and female and child labour days higher under full-time bidi activity. The average bidi-rolling productivity was slightly higher in the part-time households and especially so in the rural area. In Ullal, the average household bidi income was Rs 4053 and in Pajir Rs 4467, the average being slightly higher in part-time households owing to better labour conditions in other competitive works. However, the per worker bidi income was Rs 2210 in Ullal and Rs 1966 in Pajir. This is suggestive of the fact that working conditions are better off in a semi-urban area. The per capita total income was Rs 1552 in Ullal and Rs 1219 in Pajir. The average was higher in the case of part-time households.

The next chapter compares the food, fuel and other consumption patterns. Food was the major item of consumption more so in the rural sample, showing not much difference between the different types of households.

In the semi-urban area, about 40 per cent of the households own houses, whereas the percentage is 75 in the rural area. About 40 per cent of the houses in the former and 14 per cent in the latter have been electrified. The per capita asset structure was very meagre, and more so in the rural area.

The proportion of literates was 34 to 38 per cent in both the places and only about 1.5 per cent of the literates have high school education. 55 per cent of the total workers in Ullal and 77 per cent in Pajir were union members but active participation all was minimal.

Health complications were observed among the bidi-rollers, the common complaint being asthama and in some cases tuberculosis. Per capita calorie and protein consumption was higher in Pajir and better energy efficiency was observed in the case of part-time households.

Fuel consumption constituted a larger share in Ullal and firewood was the major component. The per capita firewood consumption was higher in Ullal, where the per capita fuel expenditure was also higher and very much evident in the full-time households.

In the next chapter, certain problems faced by the bidi industry have been highlighted. The competition from cheap cigarettes and unbranded bidis, the differing wage structures in Karnataka and other states, deteriorating quality of bidi leaves over years and the malpractices adopted by some of the bidi contractors, etc. call for judicious control on the industry.

Bidi wastage has been reported at the order of 3 to 5 per cent; the quality of raw materials and engagement of child labour have been responsible for this.

The cost of rolling 1000 bidis has been increasing very much in recent years. Wages, salaries, etc. constitute about 40 to 45 per cent of total cost, followed by Central Excise duty (13 per cent). Raw materials (leaves and tobacco) account for about 20-22 per cent of the total cost. Margins to principal employers, contractors and traders vary according to particular brands and the specific trade practices adopted.

The study also considered the cooperative bidi manufacturing in Kerala, where the wage structure was slightly higher than in D.K. district. Unlike "Home-working" in the latter, factory system was in operation in former. Huge wage bill, less degree of flexibility, high degree of unionisation, dues to raw material suppliers, dependence on government contribution, etc. were some of the factors which may inhibit growth of cooperative movement in D.K. Also, the prevalent high wages and satisfactory relationship between manufacturers and bidi-rollers here have been responsible for this.

The study found out that in the semi-urban sample. part-time bidi households had higher bidi income and productivity. But the full-time households had better consumption patterns and higher saving rates. Taking per capita income as well as expenditure into consideration, all the households seemed to be above the poverty line. but among some full-timers, rendering financial help, etc. may alleviate some of their pressing problems.

It would be improper to relate quality of life to bidi-rolling as such owing to little difference in income and consumption levels between full-time and part-time bidi-rolling households; nonetheless some aspects may be related. In the semi-urban sample, part-time bidi households, having a higher bidi income and productivity seem to have a lower consumption and savings pattern than the full-time households. Whereas, in the rural set-up, the part-time units report better consumption pattern also. In food consumption. semi-urban full-timers have a lower per capita calorie consumption, while high food consumption is reported in the case of rural full-timers. There are differences in health, education and fuel expenditure between the semi-urban and rural areas; these differences are found between the part-time and full-time bidi households also.

On the whole, the levels of living in both semi-urban and rural areas demand great improvements, especially in health, nutrition, sanitation, organisation and education. In some like health, semi-urban areas would demand a better treatment. High child labour participation in rural areas would demand regulation of that labour toward realising the societal objectives.

It could be established that labour absorption in bidi-rolling is significant (especially female labour) and the conditions demand augmentation of that labour so as to increase productivity, employment and therefrom improved living conditions.

A comparison of female vs. male-headed bidi households as to decision-making role indicates that females do participate substantially or equally in some of the household and work conditions. Females (female heads) seem to take active decisions—family maintenance, expenditure, education, festivals and recreation, etc. In the male-headed households, the decisions are concentrated whereas they are spread throughout the family in the female-headed households. Working conditions indicate that there are little differences between the households.

An attempt has been made to impute the total labour time spent on various houshold chores like cooking, serving, washing, fuel gathering, water fetching, shopping, etc. In this, it is seen that the contribution of female labour is substantial. Self and household income have been compared and also expenditure on food and other items. With per capita income of Rs. 2.319 and Rs 2,424 and per capita expenditure of Rs 2,159 and Rs 2,278, the savings ratios reported by the female and male-headed households are 6.9 and 6.0 per cent respectively. Some socio-economic variables like housing, health problems, etc. are also considered wherein the situation demands substantial improvements.

Suggestions

Bidi industry provides an important supplementary activity in Dakshina Kannada. Not only that it is a direct succour to over three lakhs of persons improving their employment and income potential, but also helps to augment government tax resources and indirectly helps agriculture and other sectors associated with it. Hence, it is of paramount importance that the interest of the industry has to be safeguarded and at the same time, conditions of the workers improved.

Bidi-rolling has to be viewed an integrative part of the rural system and treated as such. It is essential that rural programmes devote some attention to development of certain sectors where diversification is possible In completely integrating the bidi-rolling activity into the rural system one could hope to realise a just treatment and its development.

The most crucial factor to be considered is the condition of child labour. The contractors tend to employ child labour since it is cheaper and easily available and that children could be kept as unregistered members so that the fringe benefits accruing to them could be appropriated by them. Basic socio-economic measures are called for complete abolition of child labour. But since this is not a probable thing to happen in the present context of the society, regulation in child labour employment has to be strengthened. In the schools situated in bidi-rolling areas, vocational education may be imparted whereby children could get education as well as training in and earning by bidi-rolling. This might apply especially to female children, who form the bulk of bidi child labour.

If a contractor wants to employ child labour, it should be only on part-time and on vocational bases, sponsored by some schools. Children could earn their livelihood, while simultaneously getting schooling. As regards utilisation of child labour at home, parents have to be convinced about the vocational aspect. When the children are not at schools, they could roll or label the bidids under the supervision of their parents or others. For this, they should get their due share in wages, which could be kept for their welfare needs.

Female labourers play an important role in bidi-rolling. To safeguard their interests, proper health education has to be imparted. As it has been found that a majority of bidi-rollers are illiterate, healthcare should be started with basic education. Adult education centres may be encouraged to impart necessary education to the illiterate bidi-rollers so that they can properly look after their occupation, household and children.

Health visitors should periodically visit the families and help the workers toward having a better health standard, they should be also appraised of better nutrition besides sanitation. The bidi manufacturers may start some more health clinics or revitalise the existing ones and engage health personnel to give periodical visits to the bidi households; this could be carried out especially in urban areas, where health problem demands much attention. The bidi workers may be given a stipulated sum as medical allowance.

Bidi making should be completely non-mechanised. As a matter of fact, experiments in introducing mechanical cutting of leaves and rolling failed sometime back. In some places, the manufacturers encourage mechanisation in the hope of reducing the wage bills and labour problems. Once mechanisation comes, it may be difficult to find alternate sources of employment to bidi-labourers. And bidi consumption is not growing swiftly so as to allow for a certain proportion to be mechanised. Hence, bidi manufacturing has to be completely left for cottage industry.

The manufacturers can be helped in government exercises proper control on unbranded and duplicate bidis and also by rationalising the excise duty and tax structure. A high price level for bidis would keep the demand at a constant growth rate only. Rationalisation of tax structure may induce the producers to reveal the exact quantity of production and benefit-accrual to the bidi workers, thus improving the capacity of the industry. Also, supply of quality tobacco and bidi leaves in time would improve quality and productivity at the same time reducing wastage of raw materials. Speedier, steady and cheap means of transportation, better storage facilities not only in establishments but also in houses would be additional factors in this.

Though the concept of cooperation helps in reducing exploitation by the manufacturers, it does not solve all the problems. If a cooperative society is established, it should not face raw material problems. Also, there could be some flexibility in the employment of home-workers. If some workers, to avoid the exploitation by sub-contractors, come together to form a cooperative society, they may find it difficult to install a factory and obtain other requisites. On experimental basis, if some contractors are done away with and in their place, cooperative societies are introduced, the workers may buy raw materials from the society, do "Home-working" in rolling and then hand over the produce to the cooperative society. The society, in turn may forward the bidis to the manufacturer—private or cooperative.

Caution has to be exercised in trying an experiment of this type, since the existing system is not a disgruntled one according to experience. But the point is that majority of the workers feel "Home-working" is the most convenient and flexible type of employment, requiring very little capital investment in buildings, infrastructure, transport, etc.

"Home-working" mean a low degree of active unionisation on the part of the members. But there has to be a strong section which should educate the workers on the benefits of active participation and worker involvement in management.

In the labelling factories, the hot air treatment to dry the bidis has to be modernised everywhere, so that, it would save labour hazardness, besides providing other benefits. This is a case where labour power can be used most judiciously and healthily.

As regards full-time bidi-rolling, owing to its low opportunity cost. household total income is not maximised as in the part-time cases. So, as far as possible, bidi-rolling has to be extensive across families and not intensive (in the sense of being adopted by all the family members). If demand for bidi labour would be increasing, opening up of industrial premises in selected places may help in restructuring labour on the one hand and improvement in wage rates on the other. In such cases, the extensity of bidi-rolling concept may receive a good cause. Bidi-rolling could supplement other activities (by not becoming itself the full-time activity) and may assist to help in their growth. This would be valid more so in rural areas. For that, a diversified rural industrialisation, if infused, might slowly change the situation.

Bidi labourers have to spend a large proportion of income on food. Though most of the workers may not fall under the integrated rural development subsidy programmes, they could be nonetheless, helped by provision of foodgrains, fuels and so on at reasonable prices. Full-time housholds in the interior rural areas might demand direct assistance, owing to poor per capita income structure. In this district, rice production is insufficient and the district has to depend upon imports from other districts. This suggests for augmentation of local resources, especially irrigation, to increase agricultural production. In which case, rural labour could find a better employment base, to be supplemented with bidi-rolling. The poorer sections of bidi workers may be helped by the integrated rural development programmes to augment their other part-time activities.

Through I.R D.P or other means, the housing problem of the bidi workers has to be tackled. Since most of the workers (especially in semi-urban set-up) live in uncongenial and rented houses, liberal assistance might help them to own house most convenient to carry on bidi-rolling and other activities. This could be done on cooperative basis also.

Though the conditions of other agricultural and non-agricultural labourers may be deplorable when compared to that of bidi labour, it should be borne in mind that bidi-labour in Dakshina Kannada also demand modernisation in working conditions. In other places (even in the interior villages of Dakshina Kannada), their conditions have to be improved with greater emphasis on employment, income and other parameters. This is not peculiar to bidi workers only but falls under the large domain of restructing the rural society toward a higher level of development.

Index